DEAL WITH IT!

MASTERING 21
TOUGH SALES OFFICE SITUATIONS

BY JEFF SHORE

ISBN 1-932433-59-7

Printed by Signature Book Printing, Inc.
Gaithersburg, MD

Cover design by June Steckler.

Contents

Acknowledgements

Am I allowed to list a thousand names that I would truly like to acknowledge? I suppose not. Pity. Because this book is really the collective work of sales counselors all throughout the United States that I've had the privilege to know, manage, coach, train or partner with over the past twenty-plus years.

Of course, a few names stand out, people who inspired me over the years. Shannon Nalty, my first mentor in real estate sales. Jim Suth, sales trainer extraordinaire and a truly great friend. Lisa Kalmbach, my first sales manager and long-time mentor. Eric Elder, who saw more in me than I saw in myself. Penny Johnson, who provided me with wonderful (though at times humiliating) experiences. And Jason Forrest, supposedly my 'apprentice' but who, in reality, inspires me without end.

And saving the best for last… I thank God each day for His incredible blessings, and right at the top of the list is my wife, Karen, who knows me well and loves me anyway. This book – and my love – are dedicated to her.

Introduction

THE MINDSET OF A GREAT NEW HOME SALES COUNSELOR

I'm going on the assumption that you are a great salesperson. Not 'good' or 'want to be great' – but Great! It is important that you see yourself as a great sales counselor, because your actions and behaviors will always be dictated by your self-image. If you see yourself as mediocre you will do mediocre things. If you see yourself as great you will do the things that great sales counselors do.

Great sales counselors are positive energy people. They are driven to goal achievement and they carry tremendous amounts of empathy for their customers. They constantly seek to refine their skills, never being satisfied with 'good enough'. Great salespeople know that at the end of the day they are accountable to themselves for their own performance. They take pride in the job they do, and they consider how they will improve all the more tomorrow.

Mostly, great sales counselors are inspiring. They have wonderful relationships with their peers, their friends and certainly with their customers. They are successful in the broadest sense of the word – financially, of course, but also in their relationships, their job satisfaction and their quality of life.

I'm going on the assumption that you are a great salesperson, and that since you are great you will do the things that great salespeople do. Like mastering the tough selling situations, for example. Your aptitude in facing down sales office challenges is one of the hallmarks of your own proficiency.

Over the years I've met many salespeople who see themselves as "successful". But they tend to base that success on the commission pace they are on, the car they are driving or the pricey outfit they are wearing. In other words, they've made a lot of money, so they must be successful. In fact, they must be *great* salespeople.

Not necessarily. In my opinion, greatness in sales must mean effectiveness and success *market-in and market-out*. I am not interested in those who are only successful in a strong market. In fact, if you need a great market in order to be a great salesperson, what does a weak market make you?

Great sales counselors, on the other hand, honed their skills in the strong markets in order to prepare themselves for the tougher markets. Moreover, they are both strategic and flexible in their approach to the sale. Like soldiers before a battle, they know both the strategy *and the contingency plan*. They have in their minds the picture of the perfect sale, and they are prepared to deal with the difficult situations that they will undoubtedly face.

It stands to reason that improving in your ability to handle these challenges should be a part of your professional success strategy. And the payoffs are fantastic. When you improve in your capability of mastering the tough selling situations you…

- *Increase your skill*
  Every time you face down a sales office challenge and overcome adversity you prepare yourself for the next and bigger test that comes along.

- *Increase your value*
  Sales managers don't want the constant phone call from the salesperson who needs to be rescued out of every difficult conversation. The leadership of your company will greatly appreciate your expertise in deftly handling these tough situations.

- *Increase your longevity*
  Constant adversity has a way of taking its toll on salespeople. If you are continually frustrated whenever a challenging situation arises you will find that you burnout far more quickly. Great sales counselors simply last longer because they see these situations as opportunities to excel all the more.

WHAT THEY DON'T TEACH YOU IN SALES TRAINING

If you're like most new home sales counselors your initial 'training' consisted of the following instructions: "Here's a map to your community, a key, and an alarm code – try not to get us sued." When I was first hired as a sales counselor in 1987 I was simply told to head to my assigned community and start selling.

Fortunately, I had an excellent partner who showed me the ropes (thanks, Pam) but I soon discovered that the majority of what I needed to know I would have to learn on the fly. I faced various sales office situations and I improvised as best I could. The learning curve was tremendous in those first few months (and I got my hand slapped more than a couple of times), but over time I learned the basics.

What I did *not* learn in those first months was how to master the more difficult situations that I faced in the sales office each day. When it came to things like dealing with difficult people, closing on the first visit, or even remembering people's names, I struggled.

I thought I might find the answers in the sales training sessions that my sales manager provided from time to time. It didn't work out that way. Don't get me wrong – sales training is absolutely essential and I'm a big advocate. Effective training teaches new skills, and it keeps you fresh and motivated. But for the tougher challenges the learning came by doing. Most of the difficult selling situations don't fit neatly into the 'Critical Path' training module. In fact, veteran sales counselors will tell you that they learned 10% of what they know in a sales training program, and 90% through trial and error.

It has been said that experience is the toughest teacher because you get the test first and the lesson later. That is definitely true in new home sales. So much of our "training" comes from what is learned on the job, and the greatest of those training sessions come through dealing with tough situations. Each time we conquer a difficult challenge it prepares us for the future.

The good news is that you don't have to experience all those challenges yourself. You can (and should) learn from the experiences and observations of others. You are not the first person to deal with the tough negotiator, or with the person who only wants the homesites that have not been released for sale. Others have gone before you and have learned how to master these situations, turning them into fantastic selling opportunities.

LESSONS IN ADVERSITY

I was hired as a new home sales representative in February of 1987 in the Bay Area of Northern California. The market was strong in the mid-1980's and it would only get stronger for the rest of the decade. I never lacked for sales in those early years. In fact, a good part of my job was handling campouts and managing long waiting lists.

I would have told you at the time that I was a great salesperson – and I would have meant it. I was driving a brand new BMW. I bought a new home. There was food on the table and a decent pair of shoes on my feet. By 1989 I was making more than my parents had ever made in one year – *combined.* Oh sure, I was highly leveraged and in debt, but with my income there was certainly no need to worry, right?

For those of you who happen to be familiar with California economic history you know where this story is headed. In early 1990 the real estate market began its rapid decline into a deep slump. The downturn was sudden and unexpected. The decline was head-spinning.

At first there was denial. "This is a temporary thing. The market is bound to correct itself at some point." After that came excuses. "The problem is we just aren't getting good quality traffic. We need better ads." After a short while the confidence began to erode. And then the desperation began to set in. I had to face the reality that I was not prepared for a market downturn. I did not have the skills and I certainly did not have the mental toughness.

And that is when I first learned to sell. That was, in fact, the beginning of this book, though I didn't realize it at the time. I recognized that in a strong market I could blow off the customers with the tough situations. After all, there were always more (and easier) prospects just outside the door. But in a tough market I needed to embrace the difficult challenges that my customers raised.

One of my early mentors in the new home sales business was a gentleman (and I use that term with all its best meaning) named Bill Kinnard. He was a veteran who had already seen tough markets and had lived to tell about them. Bill had a way of counseling his customers through their concerns with grace and ease. He was self-confident without being the least bit arrogant. The most important thing

I learned from Bill was that it shouldn't matter what is happening in the market – a sales counselor should always be prepared to handle the challenges of any customer in any market condition. Bill taught me that handling tough situations in a strong market means you will maximize the opportunities that come your way, and that handling the tough situations in a weak market means you will get the sales that others will not.

I was a successful salesperson right out of the gate. But I was only an *effective* salesperson when I learned how to handle some of the more tricky aspects of new home sales.

THE POWER OF EMOTIONAL INTELLIGENCE

Tough situations are, in fact, opportunities to make us better sales counselors. But that won't mean a thing if you are not willing to embrace the challenges. I've seen salespeople who crumble at the first sight of danger in a sales office conversation. I've seen others who rise to the occasion and handle the challenge with grace and calm. What separates these two?

In 1995, Daniel Goleman wrote a book called "Emotional Intelligence". This attribute can be defined as the part of our character that makes us comfortable in our own skin. People with high emotional intelligence are self-aware and self-confident. They have enormous empathy for the people around them. They are mature enough to bounce back quickly from adversity and they do not transfer the negative energy from one conversation to the next.

The power of a healthy Emotional Intelligence in dealing with tough selling situations cannot be overstated. In fact, the book you are holding would be useless to those who crumble in the face of challenges. Rather, this book is for people who see these trials as opportunities. They possess the Emotional Intelligence that says, "Bring it on!" for they know that every challenge has the potential to make them stronger and more effective.

HOW TO USE THIS BOOK

For New Home Sales Counselors

If you are on the front lines you can use this book in three different ways.

1) Read it through from cover-to-cover and highlight as you go along. Then go back and put to use the things that struck you the most.

2) Look at the Table of Contents and flip ahead to the chapter that will make the greatest impact on your performance today.

3) Keep the book on your bookshelf in your office and use it as an ongoing self-training manual. Pick one new skill to work on each week and really nail it down. Great sales counselors are notorious for driving their own self-improvement.

For New Home Sales Managers

One of the most important roles you play in your position as a sales manager is that of performance coach. You can use this book to gain ideas on how to handle the situations that salespeople bring to your attention. Keep the book on your shelf and use it as a resource.

You might also find that the book makes for good **sales meeting material**. You can go through a chapter each week and discuss the issues and suggestions.

THE CHALLENGE TO...*ME*

At the risk of appearing arrogant, I consider myself to be an expert in new home sales. But while I claim a certain knowledge about the business I do not claim to have every answer for every problem. You might disagree with some of the counsel I offer in these pages. *That's good!* Someone once said that if two people agree on everything only one of them is thinking.

I challenge you to *challenge me* on these ideas. Try them on for size. Work with the concepts and put them into practice. It just might solve your problem. Or it might get you thinking of a different solution altogether. That's great! Either way you win!

At the end of the day I want nothing more than to be a resource for the thousands of people I hold in such deep respect: the new home sales counselors in the greatest industry on God's green earth. Master the tough challenges and you'll find yourself amongst those who can prove that they are, indeed, GREAT!

DEAL
WITH
IT!

MASTERING 21 TOUGH SALES OFFICE SITUATIONS

I.

"We Need to Think About It"

Salesperson: *"Is this is a great home, or what?"*

Prospect: *"It certainly is. We really like it a lot. You bet. This is exactly what we've been looking for. Why, we couldn't ever hope to find anything better. In fact, this home is perfect in every way, and there is no reason not to buy."*

Salesperson: *"Well, what do you say we draw up the paperwork and make it yours?"*

Prospect: *"I don't know. It's a big decision. We need to think about it."*

Salesperson: *"Arggh!"*

You've heard it again and again. You're deep into the sales process and you believe you have a prospect who truly loves the home and seems very close to a purchase decision. But just when you are thinking it's time to pull out a purchase agreement the prospect blind-sides you with the most famous of buying lines, "We need to think about it for a while."

As Charlie Brown used to say, "Arrrrggggh!!!" You had that prospect in the palm of your hand. It was a *sure deal*. You were ready for the accolades from the boss, you were looking forward to writing the name on the sales report, you even had ideas about a nice dinner out to celebrate. "What do you mean you have to think about it?"

The mediocre response to this comment is, of course, "Oh, that's fine. This is a big decision. Why don't you take my card and call me with any questions you might have." You might as well put them in your car and take them to a competing sales office yourself.

The critical (and painful!) truth is that once the customer leaves your sales office they move beyond your influence and into the influence of other (and perhaps manipulative) salespeople who might be more adept in the area of closing technique. You must see this visit as your only shot at the sale, and you must progress the sale as far as the customer will allow. If they truly love the home (and why would they still be there if they didn't?) they will thank you later for being persistent in leading them in the right direction.

A healthy mindset here is to think of vacation ownership sales. There is no, "We want to think about it" in vacation ownership sales. There is no such thing as a 'Be-Back'. As a rule, people buy on the first visit or they don't buy – it's that simple. Consider adopting that same sense of urgency in order to get that sale while the customer is still in your office.

When a customer tosses a "We need to think about it" at you, consider these steps:

CREATE A RISK OF LOSS

One of the classic blunders of a mediocre sales counselor is to let a strong prospect leave the community without sensing a risk of loss. Underachievers fail to promote the idea that there is only *one* specific home and homesite that will best meet the needs of the prospect, and that as soon as the prospect leaves the community that specific site could sell to someone else. It is poor sales technique and a tremendous disservice to the customer *not* to inform them of the perils of 'thinking about it'.

> *"I understand your need to think about it, I really do. This is a big decision and you want it to be right. But it is my job to make sure you know that there we have just one homesite that will fit the floorplan you like, and if you were to leave without buying there are no guarantees. It could be sold this afternoon. I don't want someone else to buy your dream home, so let's talk this through..."*

SMOKE OUT THE OBJECTION

Whenever a prospect is slow to make a purchase decision it can be assumed that there is an objection left in the way. You are not performing at your peak until you can determine the specific objection and offer an agreeable solution.

This can be done in conjunction with the step listed above, by creating a risk of loss. The conversation might look like this:

> *"Mr. and Mrs. Gutierrez, I know this is a major decision and it requires a great deal of thought. I respect that. But I also know that you particularly liked the Barrymore plan on homesite 28. That is the only location where we can fit a Barrymore and that backs up to the open space. Once that home is sold there are no others, and I would hate to see you miss out. So that I can help you in this process, would you mind sharing with me what it is that you have to think about?"*

This approach will only work when there is sufficient trust established, such that the prospect sees you as an advocate for their interests and not a greedy sales hound. Approach this in a consultative manner and see where it leads. Make sure your body language is comforting and passive. Sit back, slow down, and be sincere in listening to their concerns.

CONTROL THE ENVIRONMENT

Should the customer persist in their desire to 'think about it' your next step is to attempt to control the location of this deliberation. You must do all in your persuasive power to keep the prospect from leaving the community. If they 'want to think about it', that's fine, but persuade them to do so on the premises.

The principle is simple: once the prospect leaves the community all bets are off. They could lose the home to another customer, or you could lose the prospect to another sales office. As Tom Richey says, "There's no tomorrow if they meet a better closer on the way home today." Once the prospect leaves the community you have ceded control. Emotion wanes and fear fills the vacuum. The prospect begins to consider the hassle of moving, the commute distance, the payments. Soon the fear becomes a powerful *deterrent* to action. And you have no influence on this thought process, because you are not in the picture.

Try saying to the prospect:

"Jack and Barbara, I understand. This is a major decision and I understand why you would want to give it some thought. But you also don't want that homesite sold to someone else. Tell you what. You want to think about it and I understand. Why don't you head back to the Barrymore model and do just that. I'll be right here if you have questions. In the meantime, I'll make sure we don't sell homesite 28 to anyone else, as long as your on the premises."

Again we are attempting to control the environment. If they are 'thinking about it' while sitting in the home they love so much, the home itself will act as a powerful selling force.

CONTROL THE TIMING

Alas, many a prospect will sometimes refuse your suggestion and insist that they need to 'sleep on it.' There is yet one more opportunity to retain some control over the decision making process by suggesting a deadline on the time they will take to think it over.

> *"I understand and I respect that. I think you are aware that when you leave we could sell that home to the next person who walks through the door, but it sounds like that's a risk you're willing to take.*
>
> *"You say you want to sleep on it and think it over. You do that. I'll call you tomorrow morning at 10:00 and get your answer. In the mean time if you have any questions please call me."*

This tactic removes the false sense of security that causes prospects to think they can take as much time as they want to make up their minds. It also lets the prospects know that they are accountable to you for their answer at a certain time.

This approach is inherently logical. When a prospect is leaving the sales office and is truly 'thinking about it', when are they most likely to do their thinking? On the drive home…over dinner…at two in the morning when they can't sleep. Providing the prospect with a specific deadline helps them to sort through the issues with far less brain damage.

The call on the following morning, by the way, sounds like this:

> *"Jack, I know you and Barbara probably talked a great deal about that Barrymore plan. Homesite 28 is still available – shall I put a sold button on it for you?"*

KEEP THEM INVOLVED

Try to sway precisely *what* the prospect will be thinking about after they leave your sales office, something that will keep them emotionally involved when the scary details begin to overwhelm them. Photo's of their new home work well, as do testimonials from homebuyers. You can also keep them involved by offering a specific task related to the purchase. Send them to a paint manufacturer website and have them think about how they will personalize the baby's room. Direct them to a great pizza place in the area. Have them take their kids to the park nearby to 'try it on for size.'

Finally, if a customer does leave the office under the banner of 'we need to think about it', it probably means you have some soul-searching to do as a sales counselor. After all, you thought you had them. You still believe you have the right home for them. So why didn't they commit?

The answer will be found in one of three buying factors. When we make a purchase decision there are always three important elements that have come together:

1) The product meets my needs;

2) I trust the organization I am dealing with;

3) I sense an urgency to buy the product today.

If any of these three elements are not in line you need to discover what is lacking and seek to plug that gap. Do you have relationship work to do? Are they not really all that excited about the home itself? Do they sense a risk of loss by walking away? Any of these questions could lead you to discover where their head is at and how to best move the sale along during the next conversation with the prospect.

2.

Dealing with Abusive and/or Argumentative Customers

Salesperson: *"I think you'll love our homes."*

Customer: *"Why don't you let me decide that, will ya'?"*

Salesperson: *"Right. So, have you seen anything out there that you like?"*

Customer: *"Yes. I like quiet salesmen."*

Salesperson: *"Gotcha. Well, I'd like to help in any way I can. Do you have any questions I can answer?"*

Customer: *"Look, we don't need you to play nice-nice with us. Just point us to the model and we'll somehow manage to find our way through the home without a tour guide."*

Salesperson: *"Alrighty, then. I guess this would be a bad to time to ask you to fill out a registration card, wouldn't it?"*

When you walk onto a used car lot do you instantly engage the sales representative? Do you look forward to learning from his keen insight and being entertained by his quick wit? Or do you clam up, fearful of what some schmuck is going to try to pull over on you?

It is not at all unusual to display a certain 'attitude' when you walk onto a car lot. Such a posture is one of self-defense, likely based on your previous negative experiences. You do not wish to be abused, so you strike first with a subtly abusive buying approach. The key question: *Does that make you a bad person?* NO! It makes you a car buyer. You are about to spend thousands – even tens of thousands – of dollars on this purchase and all you can think about are the bad experiences with used car salesmen in the past.

To some degree your customers are dealing with these same issues and perceptions. They are contemplating one of the most important and difficult decisions of their entire lifetime. The decision, they fear, will be followed by pain – pain associated with finances, moving, change, family concerns, etc. Now layer on top of that a general tendency not to trust salespeople. You end up with a customer who must take self-protective measures in the form of curt, cold, or even rude demeanors. The degree of their 'attitude' will depend upon the depth of their fears.

My overriding message to you: give 'em a break whenever you can. You don't need to put up with abusive language, threats, personal attacks, etc., but try to listen through the negative emotions, the sarcasm and the attitude to see whether their approach is rooted in fear. Fear is a normal part of the buying process, and a good indication that you are dealing with a strong prospect.

Here are some specific methods of calming down that agitated customer:

STAY EMOTIONALLY NEUTRAL

The irate customer will be looking for the opportunity to attack. When you confront an emotional customer with an emotional response *you will lose*. You cannot win an emotional argument with a customer – you are outgunned.

Stay neutral. Listen for the facts and the logic, but stay away from the customer's desire to lure you into an emotion-based confrontation.

TAKE CONTROL OF THE ENVIRONMENT

When you have someone who is visibly disconcerted you first need to isolate that person from all others who might be affected – that is, from your other prospects. There is nothing worse than an unhappy customer on a rampage around other prospects. Get them out of the sales office if at all possible. This takes them away from other prospects, but it also takes them into a more neutral setting. A negative conversation in a sterile sales office can make the customer even *more* aggravated, since they are fighting you on your own 'turf'. Take them outside, into a model, or to some other neutral place. The only exception here is if the customer is so irate that the sales counselor would fear for their own safety – that's a different subject altogether.

LISTEN INTO LOGIC MODE

When people are angry they are emotional, correct? The problem in dealing with emotionally-driven people is that you cannot solve the problem until the customer moves over to the *logical* side of the brain. The remedy is to let the customer vent – and keep on venting – until the emotional statements are exhausted. By default, the customer must then turn to the logical in order to proceed.

An example: A particularly upset customer says something really 'out there', such as, "This is the worst organization on the history of the planet." This is, quite obviously, an emotion-based statement, clearly without logic. After all, it's a big planet with a long history, right?! There is no appropriate comeback to this statement. Looking at the customer and saying "Is not!" will fail to win you the argument. On the other hand, after the customer has had the chance to vent some steam you are in a position to query for specifics, and the specifics come from the logical side of the brain.

> *"I want to help you with this issue. What specifically were you told by the superintendent?"*

> *"Do you remember specifically whom you discussed the issue with at the main office? Do you recall what department they worked for?"*

> *"When were you expecting to move in, and how did you arrive at that date?"*

If you ask these questions in a logical but caring tone the customer will see that you are intent on coming up with a solution. Remember, the solutions are always found in logic, not emotion. Get to the logical side of the brain to solve the problem.

DELAY THE CONVERSATION

There are times when a customer is so utterly disturbed that there is simply no way to hold a conversation with them in their agitated state. You might need to find a way to defer the conversation until they have had some time to cool off.

> *"I want to help you with the concern but I need to do some work on this. Can I call you at 2:00 this afternoon? By then I should have some answers for you."*

Not only does this buy you some time to solve the problem, but when you do call them back at 2:00, they are likely to have calmed down from their highly emotional state. They have since gone back to work or to some other activity and have stepped out, at least temporarily, of their emotional tirade. Given some time to consider the manner in which they spoke to you, the customer will often become contrite and even embarrassed by their tone. You might even garner an apology when you talk to them later in the day.

Of course there are limits. You do not have to put up with cursing, threats, verbal abuse, etc. There is a time to tell a customer, "I cannot have a conversation with you if you choose to talk in that manner. Why don't we talk later in the day. Or I could give you the number of my manager."

HAND OFF TO A PARTNER

As much as we might not care to admit it at times, not *everyone* will like us. Let's face it: you are likely to talk to hundreds (in some cases thousands) of people each year in your sales office. The chance that every one of those people will like you is pretty slim. It might make more sense to hand the prospect off to another sales counselor for a 'do-over'.

"You know, I fear we've gotten off on the wrong foot, and that perhaps I've given you some reason to not want to work with me. That's fine. My principle regard is for you to accomplish your goal of homeowner-ship. Let me propose this: that you consider working through this trans-action with my partner, Linda. Linda is great and I think you'll enjoy working with her. Would that be acceptable to you?"

SUGGEST THEY GO ELSEWHERE

There are times when a customer, despite your patient efforts, can simply not be turned around. They are not happy now, and it is doubt-ful that they can ever be turned around. It might be necessary to sug-gest to that customer that they should consider some other commu-nity. Make the offer politely, as it will often lead to even more agitation from the customer. But if the homebuyer is this difficult to work with *before* they've taken ownership of the home, imagine what they will be like after they move in. Talk to your Sales Manager about this one – it might be time to re-sell the home.

When you do find resolution to the customer's concerns you'll want to make certain the situation is fully and permanently resolved. Ask them directly, "Are we okay now?" Thank them for their honesty and reassure them that you are there to help with their concerns.

3.

Handling Multiple Prospects Simultaneously

Salesperson: *"Welcome to Eagle Ridge. I'm Jeff. So, you're out looking for a home. How's the home shopping coming along?"*

Customer: *"Well, we…"*

Salesperson: *"Excuse me. Hello and welcome to Eagle Ridge. I'm with someone right now but I'll be with you shortly. I'm sorry? Where were we?"*

Customer: *"Well, nowhere actually. You were asking how our home shopping is…"*

Salesperson: *"Will you excuse me for a moment? Hello and welcome to Eagle Ridge. I'm with someone right… excuse me. Hello and welcome to Eagle Ridge. I'm with…huh? Hello and welcome to… Hello and …"*

It's the weirdest thing in the homebuilding world. It doesn't matter if you only see five units of traffic a week – you'll see four of them between 1:30 and 1:40 on Saturday afternoon. This is one of the strangest laws of new home sales: customers visit in bunches. Perhaps they're all on the same bus, or maybe they all got out of the same movie at the same time. Whatever. Inevitably you're stuck trying to deal with multiple prospects simultaneously.

For some sales offices this is a common occurrence. As a new home sales counselor in Northern California, for example, I routinely saw between fifty and one hundred traffic units per week. At the time of a grand opening there are communities in the United States that will regularly see far more than that.

Whether you are in a high traffic or low traffic community you need to be prepared at any given time to deal with a rush of traffic. Here are a few techniques to keep in mind:

KNOW THY CUSTOMER – AND FAST!

One advantage that salespeople in high-traffic communities have is that they are forced to speed up their discovery process with every customer. They know that time is at a premium, that at any moment the door could swing open and another new visitor could come in. Therefore the effective sales counselors strive to learn *as much as they can as fast as they can.* They think through the order and content of their investigation questions. They don't wander off on pleasant but unnecessary tangents. They stay focused on questioning, listening and understanding.

This is a healthy mindset for *all* new home sales counselors, re-gardless of the traffic volume. Even in a low-traffic community it is al-ways possible that your next visitor is driving towards your community. Consider coming up with four rapid-fire questions that you've com-mitted to memory and can teach you important information about the prospect right out of the gate. For example:

✓ "Tell me what's most important to you in a new home – I want to help."

✓ "Do you have a time frame for when you're looking to move?"

✓ "Do you have a feel for your price range as yet?"

✓ "Why are you thinking of moving?"

SPEND YOUR TIME WITH THE PEOPLE MOST LIKELY TO BUY

This is one of the most important truisms in new home sales: always spend your time with the person who is most likely to buy. Inevitably you will find yourself in a situation where you need to make an important choice: there are two customers and only one of me – whom should I spend time with? The answer: spend your time with the person who is most likely to buy. And how do you know who is most likely to buy? By learning as much as you can as fast as you can through focused discovery questions (see above).

In the absence of a fast and focused investigation a sales counselor is forced to make a decision as to whom to spend time with based on...what? What kind of car they're driving? How they are dressed? Whether they are 'nice'? All of these are poor criteria for making such an important determination.

HOLD GROUP PRESENTATIONS

Got four buying parties in the sales office at the same time? Why not talk to them all at once through a group presentation? Not only can you save time by sharing key information just once, but you build a sense of urgency when customers see that there are others who are considering purchasing at your community. Everyone wants to buy where everyone else wants to buy. Group presentations provide a great sense of validation that this is a 'happening' neighborhood.

When you have several buying parties arrive at your sales office or model home at the same time, simply raise your voice a bit and share information that will be beneficial to all concerned.

> *"Folks, welcome to Eagle Glen. I'm Jeff and I thought while you're all here at the same time I'd give you a general overview of our community before you see the models. After that I'd be happy to answer specific questions and show you through our model homes. Eagle Glen is a community of three- and four-bedroom homes..."*

The only downside to group presentations is that it limits your ability to discover what is specifically important to the different parties you are addressing. Since there is still only one of you and four of them you will eventually need to determine whom to spend time with *first*. Be attentive to the body language during your discussion, noting which customers are showing the most interest. From time to time ask if anyone has questions. Those with the questions are more likely to be the most interested buyers.

SCHEDULE FUTURE APPOINTMENTS

If you suspect you have two strong prospects in the sales office and you can only spend time with one of them you'll want to offer a specific one-on-one appointment with one of the parties at a later time. Pull them aside and inform them of your dilemma, and ask if they can come back later in the day or first thing tomorrow – but make sure you designate a specific appointment.

> *"I'm sorry for any inconvenience but we're pretty busy right now and my attention is divided trying to handle several visitors at the same time. I'd really like to offer you my full and undivided attention. Is it possible we could schedule an appointment for later this afternoon or first thing tomorrow so I can help you without interruption? I'd be happy to stay after hours today or come in early tomorrow if you need me to."*

The offer to stay late or come in early is a sign of respect and care for the prospect's schedule, and will likely go a long way towards an agreement for a future appointment.

SEND THE PROSPECT OUT FOR COFFEE OR A SANDWICH

When I was working in a sales office we had a favorite sandwich and coffee house just a few blocks away. I got to know the owner fairly well and I set up an 'account' at the place. From time to time I would send a customer over to that sandwich shop while I was busy working with another prospect, informing them that they had great sandwiches and excellent coffee. "Tell them Jeff sent you." The employees would then put their charge on my 'tab' and I'd pay it later.

By buying the prospect lunch I bought myself some time to finish up with my other customer and to prepare for the appointment. I also bought a commitment to return. I never had a customer take me up on the lunch offer and then fail to return to my sales office. Further, psychologists will tell us that people are far more likely to do something for you if you've first done something for them. Your action in buying lunch will lead to a reciprocal act – in this case the agreement to return to the sales office.

Finally, consider investing in a stack of Starbucks cards, providing you have a Starbucks fairly close by (and these days, who doesn't?). Hand a card to a strong client when you are busy and set an appointment for 30 minutes later.

4.

Closing on the First Visit

Salesperson: *"Well, this looks like a great house."*

Prospect: *"We sure like it."*

Salesperson: *"How about that. You found a home you love on your first visit."*

Prospect: *"How about that."*

(Awkward pause, kicking the dirt, looking down)

Salesperson: *"Well, here's my card. Why don't you call me with any questions."*

Sales Manager: *"Can I please see you in my office – NOW!?"*

Let's start with some facts. When a customer is walking towards your sales office door there are a few assumptions we can make right off the bat. In the United States, the typical new home buyer follows these patterns:

1) Their home buying search takes 45 days. That's the amount of time that elapses from the time they first start looking to the time they make a decision.

2) In those 45 days they will look at eight new home communities.

3) On average, there are two model homes in a new home community in the United States, therefore they will look at sixteen model homes.

4) 68% of new home shoppers are also looking at resale, and in their 45-day shopping period they will have looked at seven resale homes.

5) Approximately 80% of home shoppers are using the internet in their home search. If they show up at your community they've likely seen you on-line, *and have chosen not to eliminate you as a viable option.*

So the *typical* first-time visitor to your community has been looking for over a month, has seen more than 20 homes, and is fully educated regarding their housing choices. *What is it about this visitor that would suggest to you they are not in a position to buy* <u>today</u>*?* Sadly, all too often the only thing that holds them back is a sales counselor who does not give them the opportunity to do so. Too many new home sales representatives believe that people do not like to purchase on the first visit, so they fail to aggressively close on that first visit. Big mistake.

This has far more to do with the sales counselor's mindset than with their technique. You must believe in your heart that the person who is walking into your office for the first time is there for a reason: *to purchase a home* <u>today</u>!

Here are four principles for you to adopt.

DON'T STOP THE SALE

Any time a new visitor comes into your sales office the sales conversation will eventually end in one of two ways: either they will buy or they won't buy. If the prospect does *not* buy it means that someone stopped the sale. It is only a question of who the culprit was – you or the customer.

For any number of reasons the customer might stop the sale. But you must *never* stop the sale. Keep that sales process moving forward towards a close. Adopt the mindset that the purchase decision is the last logical step, and everything you are doing works towards that step.

STOP RELYING ON BUYING SIGNALS

I'm a contrarian compared with most sales trainers on this issue. Sales trainers will suggest that you should look for specific buying signals from your prospects – heightened energy levels, move-in questions, etc. It's one thing to ascertain the customer's intentions and their place in the purchase process by hearing these things, but it is quite another to rely on buying signals in order to get you into 'selling mode'.

Let me use this example. I don't know whether you have ever been 'secret shopped' – where a 'mystery shopper' comes in with a hidden camera or microphone to record your sales presentation. These recordings are used as a training tool to evaluate and improve your performance. I've seen hundreds of video shops in my career – I believe they are invaluable training tools. But when I'm watching a video shop I play a little game: I try to determine the exact moment that the sales counselor suspects they are being shopped. The conversation is proceeding along when the shopper says something that tips off the sales counselor that this might be a secret shopper. Suddenly, the sales counselor's energy level picks up. The pace quickens. They start talking about the schools and they share the builder's story. They start using soft closes and they become more urgent about moving the sale along.

What's wrong with that picture? Whether the sales counselor is tipped off that they are being shopped, or whether their energy level excels based on some juicy piece of urgency information given to them by their prospect, it demonstrates that the salesperson's energy level *was not where it should have been in the first place.* Why did it take the shopper or prospect to 'perform' in order for the salesperson to give them the benefit of their positive energy and best presentation? Shouldn't they have already been there?

Folks, there is one, that's right, *one* legitimate buying signal: the prospect came through your door.

YOU'VE GOT NOTHING TO LOSE

The absolute worst-case scenario is that the customer will say 'no'. Big stinkin' deal. If you can't handle rejection you are definitely in the wrong line of work. You really have nothing to lose by closing on the first visit. You won't offend the customer because they *expect* you to close. After all, you are a *salesperson*, and this is a sales office. This is what you do and the customer knows it.

YOU HAVE MUCH TO GAIN

What are the benefits of first-visit closing attempts? First of all, you get the customer seriously thinking about the purchase. They think about it now; they think about it later. Your request for a decision accelerates their decision-making process. That's good!

Second, you make the *next* closing attempt a lot easier. The customer already expects a follow-up attempt, and both you and your customer know that the presentation is geared towards resolving the customer's lingering issues so that they can buy.

Finally – and stay with me on this 'cause I'm going to get radical on you – *they just might say 'yes'!* Really, it happens. That is, if you allow it to happen.

5.
Closing on the Fifth Visit

Prospect: *"Hello, Jeff!"*
Salesperson: *"Hello, Mr. Rodriguez."*
Prospect: *"I'm back again to look at lot 24."*
Salesperson: *"I noticed. Do you need the key again?"*
Prospect: *"Nah, I've been here so many times I had a key made on my last trip."*
Salesperson: *"Smart. Do you need anything from me?"*
Prospect: *"Nope. I'm going to make my decision any month now."*
Salesperson: *"Wake me when you do."*

You know the type – always looking, never buying. They give you all the right signals; they have a clear need, financial capability and a love for your product. They say all the things that get you to believe they are a whisker away from a purchase decision. In fact, they love you personally and have made it clear that they respect your talent and ability. They even refer to you as 'my salesperson' when talking to others. They just can't pull the trigger.

Be clear on this: the strong relationship you've built in all their previous visits won't give you any comfort when they finally decide to proceed…*with a competitor.* For the frequent visitor / reluctant purchaser you have to do some important and urgent soul-searching. You must ask yourself whether the cause of the delay is your lack of assertive closing?

This leads is to one of the more important questions a new home sales counselor can ever ponder: "Is closing something I do *to* someone, or is it something I do *for* someone?" How you answer will determine your course of action with this prospect.

Why is the question so important? Because if you see closing as something you do *for* rather than *to* a prospect, you will actually close this type of buyer more assertively. Why? Because the longer they wait the harder the decision becomes. You are not doing them any favors when you elongate the process by not closing as strong as you should. In fact, you are likely adding to their brain damage.

Moreover, you need to face an important fact: after the fifth visit it's all but over. The longer this process goes on the more the buyer's urgency wanes – and no urgency means no sale. As time goes by your customer falls into a pattern of delay, and they find no loss in doing so. Eventually that initial positive emotion subsides and they are left with a jumble of facts. In other words, the longer the process goes the more logic-oriented it becomes. That is not good.

So what are we going to do about it? Here are three approaches to consider:

PUT ON THE "COUNSELOR'S" HAT

I favor the title of 'sales counselor' for new home salespeople because this is the most important role we play. You must counsel your customer into a purchase agreement.

As a counselor, you must first determine the root of the hesitation. Principally, you must discover whether the delay is based on fear (emotion) or event (logic). Fear delays include concerns about making a commitment, indecision between two different homes or neighborhoods, or financial unease. Event-based delays are easier to deal with once you discover the cause of the inaction: gathering funds, selling their current home, school timing, etc.

If the customer has come in several times without purchasing (despite your persistent efforts) you'll need to ask some pointed questions in order to determine the root cause of the procrastination. By this point you should have built enough of a trust relationship with the prospect to be blunt and direct.

> *"Mark, you've come in several times and you've indicated that you like our homes and our community, yet you have not purchased. I need to understand what's going on in your decision-making process. Tell me why you haven't moved forward with a purchase decision on the home that you clearly love."*

Then listen attentively and respectfully to the customer's concerns. This is not the time for judgment on the merits of their delay. Rather, it is time to counsel them into a breakthrough moment.

MORE CLOSES MEANS STRONGER CLOSES

I'm going on the assumption that you are a professional, and therefore you are not satisfied with having asked for the sale just one time. The true sales expert will take advantage of closing opportunities throughout the follow-up process. The good news is that once you've asked the customer for the sale they'll expect that you'll ask again. The closing process becomes easier with each close.

But with the slow-mover you must be more assertive with each of your closing approaches as you progress through this process. You have permission to become more frank with your closes on each subsequent attempt. Not rude – but right to the point. By the fifth visit there is no need to soft-pedal the question.

"Jose and Sabrina, this is the fifth visit to the home that you clearly love. Most people would have long-since put this home under contract. You know you love it. Why not make today the day?"

"Mandy, you know you love this home and you know that we will eventually sell it to someone. You don't want us to sell your dream home to someone else, do you?"

FORCE A FINAL DECISION

The longer this process goes the more your chances of getting a sale diminish. Eventually the customer will simply wear out under the weight of the decision-making process and stop coming in altogether. You've got nothing to lose by forcing the customer's hand and asking them for a *final* decision: yes or no.

The reality is that you'll be doing this customer a favor. They don't need the mental anguish of delaying the decision. They need to decide to purchase or decide to move on. They might just need someone to put it to them that succinctly.

"My friends, I'm going to do you a favor. The longer you wait the more difficult this process becomes. I'm going to ask you to make a final decision in the next 15 minutes – yes or no on this particular home. Either way, I will support your decision. But you're giving yourselves a migraine by waiting too long. Either you're going to buy this home right now or you're willing to walk away and let someone else own it. 15 minutes. I'll be right here."

That might sound abrupt, but you'll find that your customers are liberated when they know they've made the final decision. By letting them know that you'll support them either way you are telling them that in your heart you want them to make the right choice.

6.
Closing when a Decision-Maker is Absent

Salesperson: *"So, you like the home?"*
Customer: *"Yes."*
Salesperson: *"And you think Bob will like the home?"*
Customer: *"I'm sure he will. And he trusts me. In fact, I bought our last home without him there and he loved it."*
Salesperson: *"Great. Bring him out to take a look and we'll see what he says."*
Sales Manager: *"CUT! Your line is, 'Would you like to buy this home?'"*

In all my years in the new home sales business I've rarely seen anything that will cause a sales counselor to bail out of the closing process quicker than the discovery that one of the decision-makers is not present. This sole piece of information will cause more than a few salespeople to reach for the 'abort' button, reasoning that this decision is too monumental to take place in the absence of the significant other.

This thinking is extremely dangerous because the salesperson's assumption becomes self-fulfilling. That is, if you truly believe that a person will not make a purchase decision under these circumstances you will alter your presentation to match your belief. The sale will never stand a chance. This is particularly frustrating to sales *managers* given the fact that sales are made in the absence of a decision-maker every day across the country.

Now, you might be thinking to yourself, "I would never buy a home without my significant other present, nor would I want my significant other to buy a home without me there." Fine, but who said you were the buyer? Plenty of people see things differently, and it is their opinion that counts.

Who might buy unaccompanied?

Relocation buyers. The husband is being transferred, for example, because his company is moving to another state. He is tied up in the business move so she makes the home purchase decision without him. Or he buys when he is in town on business and she sees the home later. Happens all the time.

"Whatever makes you happy" buyers. She has her ideal dream home in mind. He couldn't give a rip as long as it has a three-car garage. She buys and lets him know.

"Know what they want" buyers. Sometimes two people have been looking for a long time and they know how the other thinks. When they come across exactly the right home in exactly the right community it is not necessary to have the significant other present. This is a done deal. Write it up.

Dominant buyers. In many cases there is one dominant decision maker and that's just the way it is. This person will make the call when they see the right thing. Period. End of story.

Impulsive buyers. Some people are mildly impulsive. Some are radically impulsive. I have a friend who got shut out on the purchase of the home he really wanted. After leaving that sales office he passed by a different new home community. He went in, saw a home he wanted, and bought it on the spot, without so much as a phone call to his wife. Now, for some of you men that might be 'a little troubling' to your wife. But once again, you are not the buyer. If the prospect wants to buy, by all means sell!

Here are four ways to approach this sometimes difficult situation:

ASSUME THE SALE

First and foremost, assume that this person is going to buy whether the significant other is present or not. This is one of the most fundamental principles of successful new home salespeople in the country – they fully believe that *everyone* who comes in the door is there to buy a home. Let them come back to you and stop the sale, if necessary, but don't stop it for them and don't give them the opportunity to bail because of *your* bias against selling in the absence of a decision-maker.

DETERMINE AUTHORITY

When you get to the closing questions, be direct in determining the limits of authority of the prospect in front of you.

"Are there any other decision-makers in this process, or are you prepared to move forward by yourself?"

"Does your husband need to be here to make a purchase decision, or is he comfortable with whatever your choice is?"

"Are you making the purchase decision on your own then?" (You'll be surprised how often this is the case.)

WRITE "SUBJECT TO…"

If you must, write the contract subject to the approval of the significant other. This is never my first choice, because the 'subject to' makes for a lack of commitment. Also, check yourself to make sure you aren't employing this option just for the purpose of not closing on the single buyer. That said, this is better than not getting any decision at all. There is still a healthy measure of commitment that takes place when a home is held pending the approval of a spouse.

If you do get a 'subject-to' decision you must realize that the selling process is not over. Query the present buyer as to the absent buyer's hot buttons and motivations. Provide the present buyer with some selling messages to share with the absent buyer before he/she comes out to see the home. You want that person excited before they see the home for the first time.

EXPLAIN THE RISK OF LOSS

This is the most effective way to sell when someone is absent, by explaining that the *absent* person will miss out on the perfect home if the *present* person does not proceed today. Building a risk of loss leads people to get off the fence and make the difficult (but proper) decisions.

7.

Dealing with Language Barriers

Salesperson: *"This home has a spectacular entry foyer with a cathedral ceiling and a sweeping staircase that speaks only of elegance. I think you'll agree that the towering volume as you enter is stirring yet graceful, harkening back to classic architecture from a bygone age."*
Prospect: *"I no understanding this word: home."*
Salesperson: *"This could take a while."*

Let's put this one in perspective. Your spouse has been offered the perfect job doing exactly what they've always dreamed of (and making *huge* money). It's the perfect opportunity – and the only sacrifice on your part is that the job is in *Guadalajara, Mexico*! So off you go on a house hunting journey. (All right, I can hear the retort of "So long, honey. Don't forget to write" – just go with me on this!). You're feeling mighty confident when you walk into that new home sales office, aren't you? This is where those three years of Spanish One will really pay off, right? And you know all about the purchase process in Mexico, and the financing process, and how to determine good quality, and how to know if you're getting ripped off...

Welcome to the perspective of so many people in the United States today. Buying a home is tough enough, but without really knowing what you're doing it becomes ten times tougher. So many customers have not mastered the English language. They are not comfortable with the oddities of the American culture. There is a lack of trust based on a lack of familiarity. Bluntly, they are scared – just as you would be if you walked in their shoes.

This makes for a wonderful and untapped opportunity for you - a hidden market, if you will. What do these prospects need from you more than anything else in the world? Think about that last question for a moment and try to come up with an answer. What these prospects need more than anything else is a sales counselor they can trust – one who truly cares about who they are as individuals and who is willing to patiently work through the communication gaps. You can cement their loyalty (and the sale) with a little bit of patience.

My advice is to specialize in this buyer. Establish yourself as the one sales counselor who will go out of the way and take a little more time to make this customer comfortable.

Here are a few techniques to consider when dealing with this prospect:

SLOW DOWN!

I took four years of Spanish in school and I felt I knew a few things about the language. I could conjugate verbs like a madman and I had no trouble ordering food in a Mexican restaurant. Later I got the opportunity to use what I had learned while working with a number of Spanish-speaking people. Man, was I lost! I could pick out perhaps one quarter of what I heard. I learned Spanish at a slow speed, not the way it is spoken by natives.

This is absolutely the case with so many of your customers. They cannot trust you if they do not understand you, and they often cannot understand you until you slow down and allow time for mental interpretation to take place.

Better yet, give them *permission* to slow you down. Tell them to stop you whenever they don't 'get it'. One way to do that without offending them is to take a self-effacing approach:

"You know, I have a tendency to talk too fast at times. If we ever get to the point where I'm talking to quickly for your comfort, please let me know. It's something I'm trying to work on."

TAKE AN INTEREST IN WHO THEY ARE

I was in a taxi in Denver, Colorado recently and I struck up a conversation with the driver. I wasn't expecting anything more than casual banter, but I discovered within 15 minutes that this man was a guerrilla fighter in Ethiopia in the 1970's; that he trained guerilla warriors both in Ethiopia and Sudan in the 1980's; he escaped Ethiopia leaving everything behind – including his family; and that he now drives a cab only to save enough money so he can go back to Ethiopia and Sudan as often as possible, sneak in and out, and plant churches in those two countries.

What an amazing story! I was enraptured and humbled to hear his life story. And to think I almost didn't bother to ask anything about this fascinating man. The key to this story is that despite his difficulty with the English language (I had to fill in the gaps from time to time), my interest in him made for an unusual and enjoyable bond between us.

The mediocre sales counselor seeks only to *tolerate* those who struggle with the language. The great salesperson reaches to a deeper level than the language, seeking to discover something about this visitor's soul that will spark a trust relationship. Your homebuyers have incredible stories to tell, stories of success, failure, heroism, war, travel, poverty, personal endeavor, family values and much more. All they need is for you to take an interest. Do it – and be prepared to be surprised.

I almost hate to say it for fear of encouraging manipulation, but when you reach out to the language challenged you increase the trust level so remarkably that you greatly increase your chances of getting a sale. So many sales counselors will not go out of their way to take the time with these customers; this becomes an untapped buyer resource for the caring sales counselor.

CHECK IN FREQUENTLY DURING THE CONVERSATION

Consider memorizing a simple, four-word sentence and using it frequently throughout the encounter. The phrase is, "Does that make sense?" You should be constantly checking in with the prospect to make sure they are 'getting it'. Many customers are self-conscious about not being able to keep up and are therefore unwilling to let you know that they've missed something. When you ask them if what you are saying makes sense you are giving them permission to slow you down.

Keep in mind that this technique is not limited to those who struggle with the English language. This is a good habit for any sales-person to use with any customer.

ELIMINATE 'BUILDER SPEAK'

Consider for a moment how difficult the English language is. It's tough enough without throwing in all the builder-ese terms that are entirely unfamiliar to your customers, especially to those from other cultures.

For example, you're walking through a home and you casually

point out the bull-nose corners on the walls. Now, your foreign customer knows the word 'bull' and he knows the word 'nose', so he puts them together just as you've said. Does this make any sense whatsoever? Of course not. Try then to explain how mortgage insurance works, or what an "APR" is, or a supplemental tax assessment.

It is far too easy to lose a customer while we rattle off our presentation in builder-ese. It is imperative that we stop and check in on a regular basis to allow the customer to ask questions and slow us down.

"Does that make sense?"

"I know that can be a complicated issue; are you clear on all this?"

"Do you have questions about that?"

Keep in mind that this principle does not only apply to those who struggle with the language but to anyone who is unfamiliar with terms that you and I might consider to be common in the industry. Be cautious when you are dealing with first-time buyers, for example. A couple might be purchasing their first home and to them the word 'elevation' has always meant just one thing: how high am I above sea level? Suddenly the word is inserted into the sales presentation in reference to the architectural style and confusion sets in.

This is also common with terms that describe the elements in the home: landing; pony wall or knee wall; soffit; PUD; "Good Faith" Estimate (are other estimates in "Bad Faith"), and so many more. You don't want your customer to feel stupid; be careful with this.

WORST CASE: ASK FOR AN INTERPRETER

I'm not in love with this idea, simply because it requires that any interpreter convey not only the message but also the trust I am attempting to build. But this is preferable to having a customer who simply does not get it, nor will they likely *ever* 'get it'. You might want to talk to your sales manager first, but when you sense that your words will not be understood you must be aware that the customer will inevitably end up with a confused version of the process. This is a good time to call for help.

There is one more consideration that shouldn't be overlooked. The network of people who come to the United States from other countries is stronger and wider than you might think. In most cases, Vietnamese-Americans know other Vietnamese-Americans in their geographic areas. The referral possibilities are incredible. If you can get your homebuyer to share the message that there is a great community of homes being sold by a trustworthy sales counselor, you can corner that referral business.

That said, spending extra time on the language-challenged buyers is what you should do simply because – well, it's the right thing to do. These people need your help and your patience is your gift of customer service.

8.
Helping a Customer through "Buyer's Remorse"

Salesperson: *"Hello, Frank. Hi, Marcia. How can I help you?"*

Prospects: *"We had a question for you."*

Salesperson: *"Shoot."*

Prospects: *"When you said three hundred thousand – did you mean three hundred thousand dollars? Like, American dollars?"*

Salesperson: *"Uh, yeh. What did you think I meant?"*

Prospect 1: *"Well, that's what we thought you meant. But then we got home and started thinking, if we need to stop eating out in order to buy this house, and if we spend $50 a week eating out, that means we can't eat out again for another 115 years."*

Prospect 2: *"And five months."*

Salesperson: *"We'd better go back to square one here."*

Just how real is buyer's remorse? Is it a natural occurrence, or have we projected this fear into the customers' minds? Is this something that needs to be addressed up front, or should we wait until we see signs of a possible cancellation?

There are a number of opinions on these questions, so let's look at what the customer is going through in the process of buying a home to see if there are some clues as to the validity of this phenomenon.

THE CUSTOMER'S FEARS:

- ✓ Fear of change. This is one of the most serious issues that a customer will ever deal with, and it can have a crippling effect for some people. This explains why so many people don't move at all, rather than uprooting all that is comfortable in their lives.

- ✓ Fear of commitment. The mortgage payment is like an unrelenting clock that just keeps chiming. If I don't like the home I am renting I can simply give notice and move out. It's not so easy once I own the place.

- ✓ Fear of loss. Everyone expects their home to appreciate, but everyone knows that housing prices can go down. A customer who had saved for five years to come up with the downpayment risks losing all that hard-earned money if market values retreat.

- ✓ Fear of a bad choice. There are so many decisions out there. Buy or rent? New or used? Builder 'A' or Builder 'B' (or 'C' or 'Q' or 'Y')? Lot 24 or lot 39? Elevation A or Elevation C? I could go on – we've only scratched the surface of the number of choices to be made. The shear volume of choices makes for a difficult night's sleep, with plenty of time in the dark to reconsider each decision.

- ✓ Fear of being taken advantage of. No one wants to look the fool. No one wants to find out later that the smooth-talking salesperson was actually a shyster. They trust you now, but will you still be there for them down the road?

✓ Fear of the unknown. This might be the most disturbing and distressing of all the concerns of a homebuyer. The issue is not whether the buyer has all the right answers. The real concern is that they don't even know the right *questions*. So much of homebuying is a great mystery. Within this understandable ignorance lies a great deal of apprehension, and left unattended these fears can lead to a cancellation.

Look at that list and put yourself in the customer's shoes. These things are real, and they are shared in part or in whole by every homebuyer in the world. Yes, "Buyer's Remorse" is a very real malady that must be dealt with. Here are a few suggestions:

EDUCATE THE CUSTOMER

Your customer needs to know how common 'buyer's remorse' is. Let them know that they are not alone in what they are experiencing, and that all homebuyers go through this to some degree. Then share a third-party story about another couple that experienced remorse but decided to hang in there and by the home they love.

You can also use the opportunity to remind them of all the positive reasons they decided to purchase in the first place. When they made the decision they were in love. Why? Connect them back to that point and remind them of what it was about the home and the community that was so appealing.

GIVE THE BUYER A WARNING

It's okay to warn your customer at the time of contract that 'Buyer's Remorse' really happens, just as it happens with every major decision we make in life. Most everyone who gets engaged, for example, has at least *some* second thoughts about the permanency of marriage. The decision to purchase a home is one of the most important choices we will make in our lifetime – of course there will be second-guessing. That evaluation time allows us the opportunity to further cement into the logical side of our brains the conviction that we have made a good choice.

> *"I want to warn you that some – not all – but some people who buy a home (or a car or a boat) deal with a questioning period just after the sale has been made. This is a natural and even healthy occurrence. Don't fight it. Just do two things. One – remember why you bought the home in the first place: You love the location and you went nuts over the kitchen. Two – call me and share your concerns – it's helpful to talk through whatever is on your mind. Don't be surprised and don't worry about it. It's natural."*

INFORM THEM OF THE CONSEQUENCES OF CANCELING

Too many sales counselors make the mistake of threatening to kept the customer's deposit only after the buyer has threatened to cancel the transaction. Sorry, but that's too late. By the time the customer is threatening to walk they have already become emotionally detached from the home, and once that happens there is little to be done.

The secret is to firmly instruct the customer as to the consequences of a cancellation *while they are emotionally tied to the home,* that is, at the time of the contract. Don't be wishy-washy and don't give them a hint that they can walk away without recourse. You are trying to instill this consequence into their minds so that in the event they consider backing out they will immediately consider the financial risk.

> *"All right, folks. You love the home and that's great. We're glad you love it, and we're going to build you a wonderful home for your family. You are committing to buy it, and we are committing to build it for you just as you instruct us. We are moving forward with the full intention*

of building you a quality home. That's our commitment and we are putting it in writing. Your commitment in writing is that you will go through with this purchase. Should you at any time decide not to go through with the purchase you would be going against your contractual obligations, and I want to go over with you now what the financial loss would be in that event."

Warn them regarding keeping the deposit before you have to do so. Bringing up the deposit after the final decision to cancel rarely leads to the customer "un-making" that call, since by that point the emotional tie has been severed.

RECONNECT WITH THE EMOTIONS

When a customer hints that they are having second thoughts over the purchase you'll want to take them back to the emotional place where they were when they decided to buy. That decision was made at an emotional high point in the interaction – they had fallen in love with a home and a homesite. Try to recreate that in a description. Refresh their minds as to why they made the decision in the first place.

"Thanks for sharing your concern with me. I really appreciate you bringing it up and I want to help you through this very normal process. You say you're concerned about the financial commitment, and I understand that. Can we for a moment go back and revisit the reason why you chose this home in the first place? Tell me some of the key reasons why you decided to purchase..."

"Thanks. So, you'll agree that those things that attracted you to the community have not changed, right? And the financial issues have not changed, right? Yes, I understand it's a lot of money, but you need to consider the fact that you are buying a home – a home that is just right for your family. When you go through with this decision you are reaffirming that you've done something wonderful today that will positive-

ly affect you for years and years to come. Tell me how you're feeling."

BUY SOME TIME – (GIVE THEM A CHANCE TO FALL BACK IN LOVE)

Your customer made an emotion-based decision to purchase the home. That's good. What you don't want is for the customer to make an emotion-based decision to *cancel* the transaction. Fear-based cancellations are painful because the customer rarely makes a good decision under stress.

Try to get your customer to take the time to allow the emotion to subside and balance it with logic. This is where the 'Ben Franklin' approach is so powerful.

"You don't want to make a long-term decision based on a short-term concern. This is too big a dream to give up over something temporary. This is what I'm going to suggest you do: Sit down with a piece of paper and draw a line down the center of the page from top to bottom. On the left side list all the positive reasons you should go through with this purchase as you had originally decided. Then on the right side list all the logical reasons why you should not. I think you'll find that the positives far outweigh the negatives."

You've probably noticed by now my affection for the title of 'Sales Counselor' as the most apt description for new home salespeople. Nowhere is this title more appropriate than in dealing with people who are thinking about walking away. This is where our role of counselor comes in to play and helps us to act in the best interests of both our company *and* our customer.

STAY ON THE HIGH ROAD

If they are destined to cancel, don't burn bridges. Ask for permission to stay in touch so that you will be their builder of choice when they decide to go ahead with a purchase. If they are going to walk away for legitimate reasons you want them to walk away with a favorable impression about you and about the company. They're going through a difficult time as it is. They don't need the added guilt trip on their way out.

9.

Breaking Through to the Under-Communicator

Salesperson: *"So tell me what you're looking for in a new home."*

Customer: *"Something nice."*

Salesperson: *"Yes...well...we'll see what we can do. Are there any features that are particularly important to you?"*

Customer: *"The bathroom."*

Salesperson: *"Right. Fortunately we have those. Let's do it this way. Would you like a one-story house or a two-story house?"*

Customer: *Shrug*

Salesperson: *"Do you have any hobbies?"*

Customer: *"I rather enjoy Toastmaster's."*

We would love it if all of the visitors to the sales office were warm, engaging, gregarious and easy to communicate with. The reality is that the sales office is an intimidating place, or at least it is perceived as such by the wary home shopper. When a customer fears a negative environment they often strike a self-protective pose which can be seen in any number of portrayals. They might seem passive, quiet, disinterested and even mean at times. Does this make the home shopper an unfriendly *person?* No! It makes them a home shopper.

To illustrate the point let me take you back to one of the least favorite locales for most people: the car lot. The majority of people experience anxiety when approaching a car lot, fearing that they are about to be confronted by an unscrupulous car salesperson whose only goal is to take advantage of them. Is this always the case? Of course not. But the fear is real and the reaction to that fear is also very real.

I like to think of myself as a 'good guy'. I don't have a lot of enemies (of which I am aware!) and as much as possible I like to get along with those around me. However, when you see me walk onto a car lot I get quiet, reserved, disinterested and unsocial. You might even read me as a bit mean. Does this make me a mean person? No! It makes me a car buyer. I know the pain of buying cars from people who have purposed to take advantage of me, and I have no desire to become the victim of another manipulative smooth-talker. My biases and perceptions control my actions.

That's how I get when I walk onto a car lot – and I am a normally outgoing person. Imagine how this response is multiplied with someone who carries these same fears *and* can be described as an introverted personality. Small wonder that customers will choose to under-communicate. This is simply a defense mechanism.

The solution will be found under one overriding concept: respect, and by that I mean *unilateral* respect. Many people will offer respect only after they receive it, but in the new home sales office we must understand that respect is earned, not handed to us. The great sales counselor will make a decision – even before the customer walks through the door – to offer unilateral respect and appreciation for this visitor. If the respect is not immediately reciprocated the mature sales counselor responds internally by saying, "That's fine – I have work to do to build the trust with this customer and earn their respect, but I will not allow my respect for them to wane in the meantime."

Respecting someone who does not (yet) respect you takes a great deal of maturity and confidence, traits that can be described as 'emotional intelligence'. Emotionally intelligent sales counselors practice unilateral respect, friendliness and kindness. They understand that what the customer needs above everything else is an advocate who truly understands what they are going through, and who will go out of their way to meet the customer's needs.

How do we do this? A few suggestions…

RESPECT THE NEED FOR CONTROL

One of the greatest fears of any home shopper is the fear of losing control to a manipulative salesperson. This customer wants to be in control, but they don't always know how. They fear that if they tip their hand and share too much information they will weaken their position.

Under-communicators need to be talked to in the language of esteem. Don't be afraid to take a submissive posture in your desire to help.

"It is my job to give you the information you need to make an intelligent decision."

"I promise to provide the best service I can throughout this process."

"I want to be a resource for you, regardless of where you eventually purchase."

MATCH THEIR ANALYTICAL SIDE FIRST

Under-communicators don't need sales counselors who are fresh out of a Zig Ziglar seminar and desire to carry the entire transaction on their own emotional shoulders. They need a chameleon, someone who will adjust to their style and their communication preferences. Does that mean we take all the emotion out of the sale? No way. It simply means that we start with the logical and factual and then transition to the emotional when the customer reaches a comfort level that allows them to do so.

Do this by sharing information early and immediately asking questions about whether you have what they are looking for.

"We have everything from three to six bedroom homes. What were you looking for?"

"We are located in the town of Orange Park. Are you familiar with this area?"

"Our homes start in the mid-$300's and go up to just under $400,000. Is that the price range you were hoping to find?"

Once it appears that your product might fit their needs, begin to transition to confirming statements *("Wow, this home sounds like it meets your needs exactly.")*.

USE YOUR TOOLS

The sales office is full of wonderful and positive distractions that will temporarily take the focus off of the one-on-one relationship between buyer and seller and instead direct the prospect's attention to something more tangible and analytical. Aerial photographs of the area are awesome for this purpose. Show them the surrounding area in full color. Blueprints too go a long way towards getting the under-communicating prospect involved. You'll find that the level of detail in the blueprints will provide a pleasant distraction for the prospect, and in that time you will often find them warming up to your presentation.

APPEAL TO THEIR INTELLECTUAL EGO

The cynic would respond, "Do you mean patronize this buyer?" Well, yes – if patronizing means to meet them at their level and understand what they are going through. Tell them you appreciate their style, and that they obviously know what they are doing. It's o.k. to say to an under-communicator, "You're in charge. I'll give you information, but you will make the decision."

10.
Bring a Once-Hot Prospect Back to Life

Salesperson (call one): *"Hey, it's Jeff. Just wanted to check in with you and see where you're at. You can still get lot 70 if you call me today. I'll hold it until you can get here. Let me know."*

Salesperson (call two): *"Hello, it's Jeff Shore. I didn't hear back from you guys yesterday and I've got someone else looking at lot 70. I know you want it, huh? Whadaya say? Give me a call."*

Salesperson (call three): *"Hi, this is Jeff Shore, you know – from Main Street Builders. You visited my office last week and I showed you lot 70, and you really seemed to like it. I um…I don't know how to tell you this but I already reported it as a sale to my manager, so I really need you to call me back."*

Salesperson (call four): *"This is Jeff Shore from Main Street Builders. We've notified the authorities and we're sending out search dogs. We're even talking to scientists who believe the planet is rotating slightly faster <u>since you fell off!</u> By the way, I got written up – thank you very much."*

Go ahead – admit it. You were already calculating your commission and deciding on where to spend it. You already told your sales manager that lot 70 was sold – you just need to do the paperwork. You even told another interested party that the sale was as good as done. And now the customer won't return your phone call. Your 'red-hot' buyer is apparently ice cold.

You should start with some introspective questions as you think back on your conversations. Were there clues that came up during the sales conversation that would have led you to believe these prospects were not as serious as you thought? Did you allow them to leave without making a commitment when they really could have done so? Did you fail to build the urgency that would have caused them to buy while they were here? What can you do to bring this buyer back?

Some thoughts on what to do now...

DON'T ASSUME THEY'VE LOST INTEREST

It's not time to give up yet. Sometimes people get busy or distracted with other issues in their lives. Perhaps they are involved in a big project at work, or their children are consuming their time over a school issue, or they have a medical concern. Remember that the whole time they are considering purchasing a home, life goes marching on. The decision might be delayed for some reason, but that does not mean they are not going to purchase at some point.

OUTLAST THEM

Homebuyers are constantly in elimination mode. This comes about in two ways: active elimination or passive elimination. Active elimination takes place when a customer actively passes over your offering for any number of reasons: the location is too far from work, the home is out of their price range, they don't like the architecture, etc. Passive elimination occurs when the home shopper simply forgets that you exist. This is why we follow-up diligently with our visitors, to prevent the passive elimination that occurs when we slip out of the shopper's memory after not having stayed in touch.

Other sales counselors will allow this to happen – you must not. Call them until they tell you to stop calling them. This is the only way to stay in their minds, and once you've fallen out of their minds you've lost the sale.

APPEAL PERSONALLY IN A MESSAGE

The very fact that you were expecting these people to purchase indicates that you had some sort of relationship established, and that relationship was based on a mutual trust and respect. If such a relationship exists it seems inconsistent that the customer would not return your calls. This might be a good time to check in with the customer to see if you've done something that violated the trust you worked so hard to build.

> *"I haven't heard from you and I wanted to make sure you left on a positive note, and that you have everything you need. I want to help make this as positive an experience for you as possible.*

Don't purpose to lay a guilt trip on them, but let them know that you thought the time spent together was meaningful, and that you are concerned that you might not have helped them in every way possible.

CREATE A SENSE OF URGENCY

I have often taught new home sales counselors to be aware of the "Closing Triangle", consisting of three elements that must be present in order for a customer to buy. These three factors are:

1) "Does the home and community meet my needs?"

2) "Do I trust the builder and the sales representative?"

3) "Do I have an urgency to act on this decision right away?"

Have you ever had the prospect who showed you all the right buying signals, who found that the home fit their needs to a tee, and who genuinely liked and respected you – but who just wouldn't buy? What caused the indecision? It was a lack of urgency. Without urgency an otherwise strong prospect will sit on the sidelines for ages.

Make certain that you are instilling a strong sense of urgency during your follow-up calls, even if you are only leaving a message. Without that urgency the customer will go on believing that it doesn't matter if they buy today or tomorrow – or next month.

Urgency builders:

✓ *"We have just two of the Madison plan left, and only one in a location that would meet your needs. You need to come by and look at what we have."*

✓ *"It's Thursday and I wanted to let you know that our price increases usually come in on Saturdays. I don't know what will happen this weekend, but it is still possible to lock in your prices today."*

✓ *"We've sold six homes in the last three weeks. You need to act now to get the best selection in the community."*

✓ *"We're releasing some of the best locations in the neighborhood on Saturday. Are you interested in picking one out before they are purchased?"*

Make sure your follow-up calls always have a tone of urgency to them. Don't leave a message unless there is an urgency element to your communication.

MAKE THE FINAL COMMUNICATION EXTREMELY POSITIVE

When you feel it is time to throw in the towel, end the communication on a strong and positive note, preferably in writing. The handwritten note goes a long way towards being memorable. This gives you the best chance of landing the sale when the customer eventually decides to buy.

(In writing): "I've really enjoyed working with you and I would be honored if you chose Sandalwood as your next neighborhood. I know you would love it here and I promise we'll take very good care of you. Keep us in mind!" "P.S. Stop by sometime just to say hello. I'd love to chat again."

11.
Dealing with the Incentive-Driven Prospect

Prospect: *"What are your incentives?"*

Salesperson: *"Well, that depends on what you're looking for. Do you have a particular home in mind?"*

Prospect: *"What are your incentives?"*

Salesperson: *"Heh, heh. You're a smooth one, you are. We've got some great deals right now. Let me take you through a model and show what you can get."*

Prospect: *"What are your incentives?"*

Salesperson: *"All right, I get it. I'll answer the question, but you have to answer a question for me first. What is the most important element in your new home?"*

Prospect: *"What are your incentives?"*

Salesperson: *"Kill me now."*

It doesn't matter how strong your market is or what other builders around you are doing. Home shoppers will inevitably ask a question that makes so many sales counselors cringe: "What are your incentives?" The question typically arises in the first couple of minutes of the conversation, and if it is not handled correctly the answer can actually serve to *destroy* the very value that the incentive was intended to create.

Let's start with a question: is homebuying primarily an emotional or a logical endeavor? Most would agree that it is an emotional pursuit that is supported by logic. What about incentives – are they emotional or logical? That depends on when they are offered. When we discuss the incentives in the first few moments of the sales conversation there is no emotional connection yet established in the offering, therefore the incentives are logical. Not good. But when we bring up the incentive *after* the home shopper is emotionally engaged in the offering the incentive takes on an emotional appeal.

In short, the earlier you discuss the incentives the less likely it is you will receive any value from that offering. The longer you wait to bring up the incentives the more likely it is you will receive an emotional return. *Keep in mind that incentives are best used as a closing tool, not as an opening tool.*

Why are homebuyers so taken with this question? For a couple of reasons. The first is that they have been trained by sales counselors to ask this question. Many sales counselors offer the incentive as a part of the price description (even when they haven't yet been asked), so the prospects believe this is a normal part of the process. The other reason the question is so common is that homebuyers have a perception that incentives (deals, discounts, specials) are a normal part of any big-ticket purchase. They take a cue from car sellers or furniture stores. Or perhaps they are from a part of the world where negotiation is so common that they expect that a "deal" will be made *any time* they buy *any product.*

Whether your incentive is $500 or $50,000 you need to protect that valuable sales tool by not playing your cards too quickly. A few ideas…

DEFER THE CONVERSATION UNTIL EMOTIONAL APPEAL IS SECURED

Think back to the last time you bought a car from a dealership. When did you talk about the price, the terms and the final deal? After you took the car for a test drive, correct? Why did the salesperson take you for a test drive before going over the terms? Because he knows that the most important factor in your car buying decision will not be the terms (which are patently logical in nature), but rather the *emotional* appeal of the car. It would be foolish for him to spew out the lowest possible price the moment you walk through the door since there is no emotional value yet established. (Nor would you accept that as the lowest price; this would become your starting point.)

We can learn something from car sellers. In fact, we can learn something from just about every other big-ticket sales organization on the planet. *Don't talk about terms until an emotional appeal is established.* When you dive too deep into a conversation about "the deal" too early in the process there is an insufficient emotional appeal established. Tie the customer in emotionally and the value becomes easier to defend.

"What are the incentives? Great question, because we've got some great terms. Let's find the home that suits your needs the best and then I'll be happy to share with you the terms on that home."

"I'm glad you asked, because I think you'll like what you hear. Is there a particular plan you're interested in? I can tell you the terms once we've established the plan you like the best."

APPEAL TO THE CONCEPT OF FAIRNESS FOR EVERYONE

We know that in many cases our buyers are dealing with the fear of *not* getting the best available terms. If you can convince the prospect that she is getting the best terms available, and that the next buyer will not get a better deal, you might alleviate some of that fear.

For most shoppers it is not a case of needing a better deal than everyone else got (though there are certainly some that fit this category). For most it is a question of whether some other customer received even better terms. Assure them that everyone receives the exact same terms (if this is the case).

> *"I can appreciate your desire to get the best terms you can get, and that is exactly what is happening. We do not negotiate on our terms, so <u>everyone</u> gets the best deal available."*

REFOCUS THE VALUE EQUATION BY REDEFINING 'INCENTIVES'

When shoppers ask about the incentives they are, of course, asking about the financial spiffs available when they purchase. But is this truly the number one incentive for purchasing a home? No! The number one incentive for purchasing a great home is….*a great home!* We need to reeducate the prospects as to what the incentive really is.

> *"What is our incentive? It's the best built home you'll find in this fantastic neighborhood – that's the incentive and that's why people are buying here. Not only that, but if you buy from us we've got some financial incentives as well. We'll get to that later."*

> *"Our incentives? A great home, a great location, fantastic schools, wonderful neighborhood amenities, 9-foot ceilings…we've got plenty. Let's take a look and I'll show you what I mean."*

TALK ABOUT MARKET FACTORS

Incentives are a function of pricing, and pricing is always dictated by the market. You might need to offer a mini economics lesson to your prospect, explaining that we set our prices according to what the market dictates.

"This home is going to sell and it is going to sell at these terms. The only question is whether or not you will be the one to purchase it."

USE THE TAKEAWAY CLOSE

Finally, some prospects just need to know that the deal could not have gotten any better, regardless of their deftness in negotiating. When you get a homebuyer who is hammering you for more incentives, don't be afraid. Your strength and confidence in your terms might be exactly what that prospect needs to see.

"You know, it appears that we are at an impasse because the terms you are asking for are not consistent with the value of this home. Perhaps you need to find a home where you can get a better deal."

12.
Remembering Prospect's Names

Salesperson: *"Hello and welcome to MarVista. My name is Jeff."*
Prospect: *"Hi, I'm Betty."*
Salesperson: *"Nice to meet you...what was your name again?"*
Prospect: *"Betty. You know, like Barney's wife?"*
Salesperson: *"The purple dinosaur is married? I didn't know that."*
Prospect: *"Not that Barney. Barney Rubble...from the Flintstones?"*
Salesperson: *"Oh, yeh. I love that show. So what can I do for you, Wilma?"*

Whether you're a veteran or a newbie in the new home sales business, remembering the prospect's name seems to be a never-ending challenge. Many of us are good at getting the name initially, but recalling it even seconds later can be a real problem. This is a critical concern given the importance of using the name in establishing a trust relationship.

We need to start with this reality: retention of any information is more a matter of the will than of technique. We'll talk about technique in just a moment, but if you are not committed to remembering names all the technique in the world won't do you any good.

The first advice I would offer is to incorporate the decision to remember the prospect's name into your 'pre-shot routine', that time of mental preparation before the customer walks through the door. In those few moments you can make the commitment to obtain, use and remember the prospect's name. That might sound simplistic, but it works. When you really want to remember something important, *you will*.

Suppose I were to say to you, "A man in a blue suit is going to walk into your office carrying a briefcase full of cash just for you. All you need to do is introduce yourself, get his name, use it, and remember it five minutes later and the cash is yours." Would you remember the man's name? Of course you would. Why? Because it's important to you. And that's the point. You need to establish in your mind that the person walking towards the door is equally important, and therefore worthy of you remembering their name.

A few hints on name recollection...

CONCENTRATE

99% of remembering someone's name comes through commitment, not through technique. Great salespeople make a commitment to those things that are truly important to the customer...like remembering the name.

Get in the habit of listening intently for the name as soon as the customer walks through the door. In fact, key in on the name so specifically that it is as if they were shouting the name at you. Single it out above all else. See the name in your mind. Take a snapshot of the customer's face and see the name written just below the photo.

You can practice this technique as a part of your normal life – at a store, a restaurant, at church, or a party.

SAY THE NAME AS SOON AS YOU HEAR IT

When you hear someone say their name you hear it externally, but when you *say* the name you hear it internally. Our words are loud inside our own head, so say it as soon as possible and you will hear it well.

"Welcome to Shadow Ridge. I'm Jeff and you are...Emily. Welcome, Emily and thanks for visiting us today." (The name is actually used twice in this example, further establishing "Emily" in the mind.)

SAY THE NAME SEVERAL TIMES IN THE FIRST FEW MINUTES

You obviously don't want to get obnoxious about this but you can use the name as an emphasis provider and thus further cement their name in your brain while showing the prospect that you are personally interested in them.

"Emily, I want to be able to point you in the right direction. Tell me what's most important to you in a new home."

"I'll tell you what, Emily. You probably want to see a model home. Why don't I get you a brochure..."

WRITE IT DOWN

If you're still struggling with remembering names you might consider taking out a guest card and immediately writing down the name on the card. This might be a bit awkward, but it's a lot better than forgetting the name just seconds after you heard it. Be honest and respectfully explain to the customers that you don't want to forget their names.

"I'm going to write that down. I meet a lot of people every day and I want to make sure I remember everyone's name – it's important to me."

ASSOCIATE IT WITH SOMETHING

Memory experts will tell us that associating a person's name with a distinguishing feature (jewelry, clothing, hairline, etc.) increases your retention. For more on this technique I recommend "The Memory Book" by Jerry Lucas. I read it years ago and found it fascinating.

GO OUT OF YOUR WAY TO REMEMBER 'UNUSUAL' NAMES

It's one thing to remember a name that you are already familiar with. "Emily? Oh, that's my daughter's name!" We can handle the Bill's and the Susan's and the Fred's. But what if the name is something less common to most people – Pushpakar or Hea or Anoop. How do we handle the names that are not necessarily familiar to us?

Start with the principle that your name can be considered to be one of the most endearing and important aspects of your identity. In many cultures the name is more than what sounds good – it carries deep significance to the family. Don't take this lightly! Go out of your way to slow the conversation down long enough to ensure that you have the name and that you can, if at all possible for you, pronounce it properly.

"I'm sorry, I didn't get that and I want to make sure I have it down. Can you repeat your name? An-NOOP. Did I say that correctly? Great. I've not heard that name before. Does it have a special meaning?"

When we are willing to have this conversation with our customers we accomplish more than just getting the name set in our own mind. We show the prospect respect and we let them know that we will go out of our way to honor their individuality. Do this because it's the right thing to do, but don't be surprised when you find that your prospect suddenly trusts and respects you right back.

13.

He Likes You; She Doesn't (or vice versa)

Salesperson: *"This backyard is perfect for parties. Do you BBQ?"*
Husband: *"Do I BBQ? Dude, I'm the BBQ king! I can cook for 40."*
Wife (mumbling): *"He can cook hamburgers for 40. I have to prep salad, make the mashed potatoes, bake rolls, cook pies, clean the house, put together seating for 40 and clean up afterwards."*
Salesperson: *"40?! Dude, you rock! You're the BBQ king!"*
Husband: *"Ya' know, I like your style."*
Wife (mumbling): *"Ya' know, I could clean your clock."*
Salesperson: *"How would you like to call this home your own?"*
Husband: *"How would you like to come over for burgers after we move in?"*
Wife (mumbling): *"How would you like a fat lip, Slick?"*

It is in the nature of salespeople to want to be liked. That's okay; you don't have to apologize for that. In fact, the desire to please is a cornerstone of effective service. After all, our customers are only pleased when they are well cared for. So when a prospect does *not* like you, it can be painful.

Take a situation where you are working with a couple; she likes you but he doesn't. You end up with a state of affairs that is both painful *and awkward*. Ultimately homebuying is a process that will require cooperation from both parties, so you'd better be able to get your hands around the situation as quickly as possible.

In my years observing and managing sales representatives I have seen that some sales counselors will handle this situation calmly and strategically, considering it a professional challenge, not unlike 100 other challenges they will face during the course of the day. Others are emotionally affected by this situation, fearing that a lack of approval is a customer's negative reaction to the sales counselor's personality and demeanor.

The difference in response of these two sales representatives is a reflection of their emotional intelligence. One has the maturity and self-confidence to see this as a challenge and an opportunity; the other disparages over the situation and allows it to hamper their own energy and enthusiasm. Success comes when we recognize that everyone is different, everyone is unique, and everyone deserves the benefit of your best efforts, regardless of whether they like you or not.

Some approaches to this situation:

DEAL WITH REALITY

You meet lots of people in your line of work, typically more than a thousand each year (and a lot more than that in some areas of the country). But let's be ultra-conservative and suggest that you'll meet 100 people in your sales office this year. Is everyone like you? No. Does everyone share your personality style? Of course not. The sales counselor who desires the immediate approval of each and every customer is bound to be disappointed. This is an unattainable goal.

When we recognize that not everyone will like us right off the bat we further recognize that relationships are a work-in-progress. It is in both the customer's best interest and in yours as well to allow time for a process of civilized conversation to develop into a trust relationship based on mutual respect, support and, eventually, likeability.

In the case of two people who are shopping together you must understand that couples are often opposite in their personalities. It is therefore likely that you will interact more comfortably with one than the other. Don't panic. This is very, very normal.

MAKE A DECISION IN FAVOR OF UNILATERAL RESPECT

If we know that not everyone will like us right out of the gate it leads us to a very important decision: do I need to respect the prospect even if the prospect does not respect me back? The answer is (or should be) "Yes"! Sales counselors with a strong emotional intelligence will make a decision in favor of *unilateral* respect. They provide their best service, their best assistance, even their best attitude to everyone who comes through the door, regardless of the demeanor of the prospect.

Understand that there are all kinds of personality types out there, and the sales approach for one does not necessarily make sense for another. Be patient and respect the boundaries of those who are less comfortable right off the bat.

"OUT-NICE" DIFFICULT PEOPLE

Suppose you are working with two people but you've only established a trust relationship with one. You must assume that the other will come along in time, if you continue to do your best work and provide your strongest service and attentiveness. In the mean time, try to "out-nice" the person.

Suppose he is acting as though he doesn't like you. This might just be a defensive posture that he takes with all new salespeople. He just happens to be more comfortable with strangers. So don't follow his lead! Outlast him with your kindness and respect. Make it your quest to bring him around.

Again, this is a *unilateral* decision. If you need someone to be nice to you in order for you to be nice to them, you're in the wrong line of work.

DON'T PLAY FAVORITES

The situation we are describing leads to a very serious pitfall for many sales counselors. "I like him, but I don't like her – so I'll be nice to him and tolerate her." Big mistake. When you pay greater attention to your favorite you will only alienate the other partner, thus deepening the problem. That other person will launch into a defensive mindset, fearing that they are outnumbered.

Think 50-50 at all times. Smile equally. When one asks a question, answer both. When one offers an opinion, ask the other if they are in agreement.

FIND A VICTORY FOR THE OTHER PERSON

Look for even the smallest things to make the grumpy person feel good. Don't overkill this, but see if you can find *something* that makes this person feel that you are looking out for their best interests.

14.

The Customer Wants Options that You don't Offer

Customer: *"Can I have my own contractor come in and do a custom wall texture?"*
Salesperson: *"No."*
Customer: *"Well, can I have someone come in and place speaker..."*
Salesperson: *"No."*
Customer: *"Well, can I at least have someone..."*
Salesperson: *"No."*
Customer: *"Can I have a..."*
Salesperson: *"No."*
Customer: *"Can I..."*
Salesperson: *"No."*
Customer: *"Ca...."*
Salesperson: *"No."*
Customer: *"Thanks for your time."*
Salesperson: *"Glad to have been of help."*

Stop me if you've heard this one: "I'm paying $350,000 for this home, and I cannot believe you won't allow me to put in a...." This is one of the most common phrases in the prospect's playbook. Can you believe these pesky customers? What's up with that, anyway? The nerve of these people – asking for things that aren't on our options sheet just so they can get the home finished the way they want it.

Okay, I'll take my tongue out of my cheek now. The fact is that buyers want what buyers want – they always have and they always will. It is only a question as to whether they will accept the fact that they can't *get* everything they want. Helping them through this education is an important role for you. It is your job to protect the company's interests *and* protect the customer's perception of value at the same time.

A customer might want a particular option that you do not offer and they might perceive this as a major disappointment, but the option was never offered to them and *they made a purchase decision anyway.* We can deduce that this is simply an objection (like so many others that come up throughout the process) that needs to be strategically handled by the adept sales representative.

How do we handle this one?

EXPLAIN THE REALITIES OF HOMEBUILDING

Homebuyers are notorious for seeing just their side of the story, not recognizing the big picture vantage point of the homebuilder. (And can you blame them? Doesn't that often describe *you* when you're considering a major purchase?) At times we simply need to expand their paradigm in order for them to understand the logical process that goes into selecting options for a new home. A few things to point out:

1) *"Everyone wants something different and unique. Speaker wiring might be important to you, but to the next home shopper it might be irrelevant – they want a wine cooler instead."*

2) *"We offer those things that appeal to the majority of our homebuy-*

ers. *We've found that when there are too many choices and there are options that are rarely selected that we run into a cost consideration – that is, not enough buyers select the option to allow us to price the option competitively."*

3) *"The more options we offer the more complex our purchasing process becomes. Complexity adds to cost, and that cost is reflected in the price of the other options."*

TALK ABOUT QUALITY CONTROL

One thing we know about homebuilding is that we cannot offer every option that every person wants and still maintain quality. The more complex the home becomes the more difficult it becomes to build it 100% correctly. Your customer must know that your company is simply not willing to bend when it comes to building a quality finished product.

We offer those items that are commonly requested and that allow us to maintain our quality standards."

"The more options we offer the harder it is to get the production process right. And we refuse to compromise on our commitment to a quality home that is built right the first time."

SELL THE HOME AS A BLANK CANVAS

There is one aspect of buying a new home that is often overlooked during the sales presentation: the concept of a new home as a blank canvas, just waiting for the customer's artistic expression to come through. Using this approach, you can swing the objection around to an encouragement. Sell the possibilities in doing to the home whatever they wish after they move in.

Let the customer know that this is one aspect of buying a brand new home that customers really look forward to. Also point out that the creation process is much easier than if they had purchased a used a home. In that case they would be stuck with the previous owners options, and they would have to undo the things they did not like before installing their own choices.

> *"One of the wonderful aspects of buying a new home that many of our homeowners have enjoyed is the opportunity to continue the customization process after having moved in. Many of our homeowners take great pride in the personal touches that no one else on their street has. You'll find yourself inviting your neighbors over to see the special addition you just installed."*

EXPLAIN THE REALITIES OF COMPROMISE

Let's get this one thing straight: there is no such thing as a 'perfect home'. It simply does not exist. Everyone compromises – everyone. Part of buying a home consists of determining your acceptable level of *dis*satisfaction – that is, what are you willing to give up, knowing that you cannot find perfection.

Because compromise is a natural part of the homebuying process we need to make sure that the customer's expectations are not out of line, and that they are not expecting to find the absolutely perfect home. Gently remind them of this reality.

> *"I know you want exactly what you want, and that's very normal. The fact is that you're not going to get <u>everything</u>, so you need to decide what you are willing to do without – at least for now. What you need to look for is the best decision <u>on the whole</u>."*

15.
Handling Price Objections

Customer: *"The price is too high."*

Salesperson: *"What exactly do you mean by that?"*

Customer: *"I mean it's not too low and it's not just right – it's too high."*

Salesperson: *"And what are you basing that on?"*

Customer: *"On the fact that the price is not where it should be."*

Salesperson: *"All right. Throw me a bone here. I want to help but you need to tell me why you think it's too high."*

Customer: *"I think it's too high because the house is overpriced."*

Salesperson: *"That was direct from the Department of Redundancy Department. Can you be more specific?"*

Customer: *"I want a lower price."*

Salesperson: *"Ah. Now we're getting somewhere."*

I have a factory, and my factory makes designer toothpicks – exclusive and very trendy. I need to sell the toothpicks I produce, so I strive to find that price that will represent appropriate value to my customers. I don't want to overprice my toothpicks because consumers would balk and I would be stuck with too much supply. I don't want to under-price them either; consumers would buy them up and I would have no inventory left to sell. I need to price my toothpicks so that customers will buy them at the exact same pace as I am capable of producing them.

Does this all sound vaguely familiar to you? If so, you might remember this discussion from Econ 101. This is the simplest explanation of the principle of supply and demand. One of the most important principles regarding pricing is that I can, at best, *guess* at the appropriate price of my toothpicks. I put my product in front of consumers at the price *I think* they will find attractive, and they respond by either purchasing or passing over. If they buy my toothpicks, I guessed right. If they buy too many of my toothpicks, I guessed too low. If they don't buy any at all, I guessed too high.

Now let's leave the designer toothpick factory and consider the application to homebuilding companies. Here is a reality that you must deal with: you are working for a *for-profit organization*. The company you work for wants and needs to make money. Your organization dwells in a capitalistic society and functions in a high-risk business. In fact, because of the risky nature of land buying, your company needs to make as much money as possible whenever it can. If the market shifted downwards tomorrow your organization would still be on the hook for the land it purchased, even if that land price diminishes.

All right, so you work for an unashamed, unabashed, financially-motivated, capitalistic company. Fine. But here is one other truth I can tell you about your builder: *your homebuilder does not set the price*. You heard that right – homebuilding companies do not set the prices. If we set the prices we would all be selling multi-million dollar homes. The buyer doesn't set the price either. If that were the case we would all be selling fifty dollar homes. It is an inescapable truth of business: ***the market sets the price***. Always has, always will. The best we can do is guess at what the market price is on a given day. Sometimes we guess too low and sell out in a few hours. Other times we guess too high and get stuck with standing inventory. The market couldn't care less one way or another. The market will determine the appropriate value of the offering and measure that value by a price. This works the same for houses, hip boots, hurricane lamps…and designer toothpicks.

Why the economics lesson? I am trying to do you a favor! You don't ever have to apologize or even defend the price of the home. We don't set the price – the market does. If the home is overpriced it simply will not sell. Period.

While you do not have to defend the price, you very much need to defend (and even to enhance) the perceived value of the home. You cannot affect the purchase price unless you first affect the perceived value. A horrible sales counselor, for example, will turn off the prospect to the offering, and subsequently the homebuilder will have to lower the price to appease the market that has been disturbed by what they see. On the contrary, an outstanding sales counselor will serve to raise the perceived value of the offering, and the company will be rewarded with a higher price.

While you do not need to argue with a customer over whether or not the homes are priced to market, you do need to make sure you fully understand the customers' value concern. As with any objection you'll want to question thoroughly to fully understand the basis for the apprehension.

Here are a few ideas on how to do that…

DISCOVER THE CUSTOMER'S PERSPECTIVE

"Your homes are too expensive" can mean so many different things. Is this a price comparison to our competition? Is this a commentary regarding this week's price versus last week's? Are they too expensive or are they just unaffordable to this prospect? Is this an issue of value judgment or of payment capability?

You must ask the questions that will lead you on a path of discovering exactly how this customer arrived at the conclusion. Here are some questions to get you started:

"Talk to me. What are you basing that value judgment on?"

"Overpriced? Can you give me an idea as to your comparison point so I can better understand how you come to that conclusion?"

"Value is a matter of opinion, and I definitely respect your opinion. So I can help you with this issue, can you tell me what you are basing your value judgment on?

"Can you define 'overpriced' for me? Tell me how you arrive at that."

MAKE A DISTINCTION BETWEEN VALUE AND AFFORDABILITY

Many people will say 'over-priced' when they really mean 'I can't afford it'. These prospects might very well agree with the value but the price is out of their comfort zone.

If this customer simply cannot afford the home, and assuming you investigated all the financing options, there is not much to be done here. But if you are dealing with someone who really *wanted* to stay under $300,000 but your homes start in the $340's, that's a different situation. I've seen people do some pretty creative things when they fall in love with a particular home.

The principle remains the same: You cannot deal with this objection until you know what it is based on.

OFFER AN ECONOMICS LESSON

Try taking the first seven paragraphs of this chapter and condensing it down to a simple explanation of market economics: the market sets the price. The more comfortable you are in explaining this principle to a customer the more likely it is you will overcome the objection.

"Value is an opinion, and so I respect where you're coming from. However, our homes are always priced to market – that is, they are always priced at whatever a homebuyer is willing to pay. It's simple – if our homes are overpriced they won't sell. But we've sold eight homes in the last five weeks. We are actually ahead of our sales pace. The market is confirming that the homes are priced correctly. It appears that the home you are looking at will sell for the price listed; it's only a question of whether you will buy it or someone else will do it first."

PROVE THE MARKET VALUE

As I stated previously, your role as a sales counselor is to enhance the perception of value at every opportunity. When a customer fails to see the value in the home it is up to you to discover where you come up short and what you might do to alter the prospect's perceptions.

"Can we take a few moments to walk through the home and make sure that I have made you aware of the special touches that add value to this home and to this community?"

16.

The Customer Only Wants the Lots that Haven't been Released

Salesperson: *"In the Marseilles Plan we still have lots 8, 11 and 15. Which would you like?"*

Customer: *"I'll take lot 22."*

Salesperson: *"I'm sorry. That's not one of your choices. 8, 11 or 15?"*

Customer: *"I really want lot 22."*

Salesperson: *"And I really can't sell it to you. Is there a specific reason you want lot 22?"*

Customer: *"I only want something that hasn't been released."*

Salesperson: *"Why is that?"*

Customer: *"Because I'm terrified of commitment but I don't want to make you feel bad, so I figure if I show a strong interest in an unreleased lot you'll feel like I'm a good prospect but I won't have to actually buy anything."*

Salesperson: *"I appreciate your honesty."*

Customer: *"In that case, I hate your tie."*

You've got a prospect who looks strong, like she might buy today. But she's favoring a homesite in a cul-de-sac that won't be released to sell for months. She is willing to wait, but you think it would be in her best interest for her to purchase a different home in a different location today. What to do?

Let's start with 'Unfortunate Reality A' – she's not a super-motivated buyer. It's easy to show interest in something you know you cannot get because the lack of availability provides comfort and escape. But we've all had situations where people asked to be placed on an interest list for a future release, only to find that these people are missing in action when the homesite actually becomes available.

'Unfortunate Reality B' says that she really does want that particular lot and that she is, in fact, willing to wait for six months, even in the face of price increases. In this case there is really very little to be done except stay in touch with updates regarding future releases.

We'll assume that this is not the case with any of *our* prospects, but we need to be prepared for anything that comes our way, so here are a few things you want to keep in mind.

DETERMINE THE LEVEL OF INTEREST

You first want to know if the prospect is serious. Would this customer actually purchase that unreleased lot if you offered it today? Ask them the direct "If I could, would you?" closing questions to determine their true interest. One tip from the pro's on this: make them absolutely commit to buying before you ask if the lot can be released. You don't want to go to your sales manager and ask for a release only to find that the customer was not all that interested in the first place.

FIND AND SHARE VALUE POINTS

Like every baby, every home is lovely to someone. Every home is distinctive and each offers a unique opportunity for the future owner.

These distinctions build unique value, assuming the customer is aware of what makes a given homesite special.

Walk the current inventory on a regular basis and find something to love about every single home. The current availability may not be perceived as better than the future offerings, but if you can stir enough interest in a location today and further motivate the buyer to purchase as a hedge against price increases and interest rate bumps, you might convince that prospect to act today.

WARN OF PRICE INCREASES

If you have a history of price increases with each phase release, share that information. If you've already been told that prices are going up on the next release make sure your prospect knows about it. Let them draw their own conclusions about what happens next but make sure there is a fear of missing out on today's terms.

Further, you'll want to refine your urgency descriptions during your sales presentation. You do not want the prospect to leave your office thinking that they are safe from a price increase for a certain period of time. Warn them that the terms you have quoted are valid only during that conversation. Once they leave the office, all bets are off.

"I can't tell you what the price and incentives will be next week. Actually, I can't even tell you with any certainty what they will be later this afternoon. My Sales Manager determines the sales price of each home, and I've seen price increases go into effect in the middle of the week. I don't know what the price and terms will be tomorrow – I only know that we have a great value <u>today.</u>

17.

Selling a Heavy Inventory of the Least Popular Plan

Prospect: *"The Winchester Plan suits my needs perfectly. I'll take the Cheyenne."*

Salesperson: *"Huh? I thought you liked the Winchester."*

Prospect: *"We do, but you've got plenty of those and you're sold out of the Cheyenne. Clearly we must be missing out on something."*

Salesperson: *"Missing something like…the best possible home for you?"*

Prospect: *"Yes, and we'd also like it on a lot that isn't available."*

Salesperson: *"And I got out of resale for this?"*

It's one of the weirdities of the homebuilding business – everyone loves the Plan One and the Plan Three and we can't give the Plan Two away…until one day for some unknown reason (perhaps tied to the alignment of the planets) everyone simply must have the Plan Two and they passionately hate the Plan Three. I've never been able to figure out this strange shift of the fates of the floorplans, but I have seen some common trends to watch out for.

The most dangerous of those trends is the sales counselor who has fallen out of love with a particular floorplan. He believes what he hears when those around him have suggested it's a lousy plan, and he has internalized those opinions so strongly that he is no longer capable of selling the home. In his book "Integrity Selling", author Ron Willingham points out that if a sales counselor does not believe that his product represents a great value for his customer, he can never reach his potential. In fact, this "Belief in Product" is so important that a salesperson cannot effectively sell the product without setting aside his own value system.

In my consulting business I have frequently come across this situation: a home or a series of homes are lagging behind in the sales column. When I query the salesperson as to the situation I'll hear something like this: "Let me tell you why this home won't sell." STOP RIGHT THERE! I don't need to hear any more. I've already discovered the #1 reason why the home won't sell – *because the salesperson is convinced that it won't sell.* In sales this is the ultimate example of a self-fulfilling prophecy.

In the above example, not only did the salesperson have a negative attitude that would prevent him from selling the home, but it is interesting to note that the sales counselor is statistically *dead wrong!* When he says that the home won't sell, that's just not true. Every home sells to someone at some point for some price.

Great sales counselors ferociously protect their own mindset, staying sharp and positive at all times. They do not allow negative talk to affect how they view their own product, and they possess the emotional intelligence necessary to bounce back when they hear comments that are less than flattering. After all, you are not selling the home to everyone – only to the person who likes it and would like to buy it.

That said, I recognize how frustrating this situation can be. Try these suggestions…

CONVINCE *YOURSELF* OF THE VALUE

Get creative and do everything you can think of to make sure you are convinced that this home represents an awesome value for someone out there. Don't let your own negative opinion rub off on perceptive prospects. Some specific suggestions:

- ✓ Walk the plan with a peer, looking for positive attributes as you go along. Sometimes a third party will point things out that you would have missed.

- ✓ Talk with those people who *have* bought the slow-seller. Ask what attracted them to the plan in the first-place, and also what they like now that they've moved in. Incorporate these stories into your presentation. Third-party testimonials are invaluable.

- ✓ If possible, talk to the architect. No plan is ever drawn as a dud. There was something special that the architect was trying to accomplish. What was it?

- ✓ Ask yourself the question, "Why will someone purchase this particular home?" Come up with an answer and incorporate that value point into your sales presentation.

EDUCATE THE PROSPECT

People fear making a mistake, especially on a major decision. Having an abundance of one particular plan might look peculiar to the prospect at first glance, but we in the industry know that this scenario is not all that unusual. Assure the prospect that this happens all the time. Some suggested verbiage:

"I gave up a long time ago trying to figure out why some homes take

longer to sell than others. I only know that selecting a home is a personal choice, and that every single home in this community will soon be sold."

"It's strange – last month everyone wanted the Plan 2. Now everyone wants the Plan 3. You never know – the Plan 2 could be the huge hit again next month."

"We only know that it always balances out in the end. We don't expect that everyone will love every plan we build; that's why we offer a variety. I'm not concerned. I know these homes will sell very soon."

LEARN AND USE THIRD-PARTY TESTIMONIALS

As I have stated previously, no one wants to be alone on a bad decision. For this reason, people seek validation from other buyers. You need to find the one thing about the plan that homeowners really appreciate, and then emphasize that value point when you are describing the home. This works best with actual testimonials from actual buyers. Call a few and find out what they love.

"The thing that people have really enjoyed about this home after they've moved in is the openness of the floorplan. I had one customer tell me how bright her living room was on a cloudy day. She was really excited."

"Everyone loves a great kitchen, and this kitchen is incredible."

Note that second example one more time. Every home has its plusses and minuses. You want the prospect to look past the potential flaw and forward to the highlight of the home. If the entryway is perceived as being somewhat weak, introduce the kitchen *even before you walk through the front door.* This gets the prospect thinking that there is something to look forward to.

MARKET TO THE QUICK MOVE-INS

Slow moving inventory usually means fast move-ins for the buyers. Get on the phone! Call your Realtor base and your relocation companies. Get them interested in a quick close.

Some sales counselors look at inventory homes as negatives, as if there is something wrong with them. Great sales representatives see that inventory homes are opportunities for just the right buyers. For the person who needs to move quickly these homes are rare and extremely valuable.

18.

Dealing with the Relentless Negotiator

Salesperson: *"That's my final price."*

Customer: *"No, it's not."*

Salesperson: *"Yes, it absolutely is. We won't go any lower."*

Customer: *"Yes you will."*

Salesperson: *"Why do you say that? I've talked with my boss and we've offered you our best price."*

Customer: *"Then talk to your boss again, because you want to sell this Plan 2 and I want the mini-blind package and ceiling fans in all the bedrooms."*

Salesperson: *"Look. I don't know how to say it any clearer. The price is the price. The terms are the terms. The deal is the deal. You've already got the best deal in the community and we're simply not going to give you one dime more. I've talked to my Sales Manager numerous times and she has made it clear she does not want to hear your name until you've signed a contract. We're not giving you the mini-blind package and we're not giving you the ceiling fans. This part of the conversation is now over!"*
(Pause)

Customer: *"Well surely you can at least do the mini-blind package, and let me tell you why I think it makes sense for you to include the fans as well…"*

Those of us with smaller quantities of hair must be careful at this point not to pull out what little we have left. The relentless negotiator is just that – relentless. And don't think that the negotiation ends with this guy just because he has signed a contract. It will be a battle throughout the transaction (and after he moves in he'll likely attempt to negotiate with the warranty representative down the road).

Consider this a test. The customer wants to know where the limits are. He wants to know he is getting the best possible deal. He wants to push the envelope whenever he can. But you need to keep something else in mind – your company is doing exactly the same thing. There is no law that mandates our sales prices. We are trying to get top dollar for our homes at all times. We put a price out there that we believe is not one penny less than market value. We all want the best terms; that's the nature of any sales transaction.

Here are some suggestions for dealing with this oft-frustrating homebuyer…

UNDERSTAND THEIR PERSPECTIVE

In the end, this prospect just wants to know is that he got the best deal he could get, that there was not one dollar left on the table. The fear of leaving anything behind can be overwhelming. In fact, when the customer believes that he could have gotten more out of the deal he will likely reopen negotiations after the fact to satisfy this disturbing curiosity.

Does this make the customer wrong? Is he a jerk because he is asking for everything? Not at all. He is the customer, and while he might cause us some frustration through his persistent badgering, we are in no position to offer a moral judgment on his character.

Before you turn to a hasty and negative reaction, take a moment to try to see things from this customer's perspective. Ask yourself some important questions.

✓ Do I have a strong sense of where this customer is coming from? Have I sought to put myself in his shoes?

✓ Is this customer convinced of the value in the home, or do I have more work to do?

✓ Is there a competitor who is 'training' the customer to ask for more?

✓ Have I done something to indicate that we will, in fact, move on the price?

✓ Am *I* firmly convinced in the value of the offering?

There is one other important consideration. In many cultures negotiation is a way of life. This is neither good nor bad – it just *is*. If you are quite accustomed to negotiating over the price of a melon at the market, wouldn't it stand to reason that you would want to negotiate over the price of the home? I have had customers who were incredulous when I told them we would not negotiate. I remember one man who simply refused to believe me; he even accusing me of lying. Eventually I turned him over to my Sales Manager, who confirmed that we would not negotiate. By the time he hung up the phone he was furious, and he walked out of my office. My guess is that he bought a different home from someone who was willing to negotiate with him. He bought the best *deal*, but not necessarily the best *value*.

Understand that you might need to offer a (very sensitive) education to the prospect.

> *"You might be used to negotiating the terms in the purchase of a home; in some areas* (note that I said 'areas', not 'cultures' or 'countries') *it is quite common. Not here. The best price you will ever get is what you've already been quoted. That might not be consistent with your experience, but that's the way we do it at this community."*

FIND THE WIN-WIN

Too many times we find ourselves on the defensive side of the ball, waiting for the customer to finish the point so that we can jump in with an explanation of why we are about to say 'no'. This is the classic symptom of an 'I win, you lose" approach. It doesn't have to be that way. You should always be looking for middle ground. Let the prospect know that you desire to help so long as they are willing to understand the company's position as well.

"You want the best terms you can get, and I appreciate that. You are aware, I'm sure, that the company has interests that need to be protected as well. So what I want to do is find a solution that works best for both of us. Let's start with a discussion on what is <u>most</u> important to you, and why."

When you can get your customer talking you will open the lines of communication and obtain a more thorough understanding of their viewpoint and their values. From there you can strategize as to where to take the conversation.

By the way, I highly recommend Leigh Steinberg's excellent book, "Winning with Integrity: Getting what You Want without Selling Your Soul". This is an outstanding book on negotiating by one of the world's foremost negotiators. The premise focuses on understanding the person you are working with as the key to success in negotiations.

DON'T FOCUS ON THE 'BEST PRICE'.

My long-time mentor, Lisa Kalmbach, taught me that what vigorous shoppers are really looking for is not the 'best price' at all. Labeling something my 'best price' is hackneyed and therefore not credible. The response is usually, "Yeh, right."

Stay away from discussions about the 'best price'; what the customer really wants to know is, "What is your *last* price?" In essence they are saying, "I am looking for the point where you are absolutely done, where if I asked for one dollar more you would turn me down and allow me to walk away." This is the 'last price', and using this term brings comfort to the customer who needs nothing more than to know there was not one dollar left on the table.

> *"I appreciate you wanting the best terms you can get, and I respect that. But you need to understand that the price I've given you is not only my best price, but it is my last price. You need to make a decision as to whether there is enough value in this home to justify this price."*

THREATEN THE TAKEAWAY

Because our customers are often consumed with getting the best possible deal they often find themselves deep into a logical analysis with the terms, all the while neglecting the emotional reasons they fell in the love with the home in the first place. When that happens, the positive emotions that caused them to fall in love with the home in the first place are diminished. You need to do everything in your power to prevent that from happening. You need to keep them emotionally charged over the purchase of their dream home, and then threaten to sell it to someone else if you cannot agree on terms.

Sometimes all a customer needs to know is that you are preparing to sell the home (their *dream* home) to someone else. Don't be afraid to be direct with the takeaway.

> *"Mr. Williams, it does not appear that you love this home enough, and that you are having a hard time justifying the price. Perhaps you need to be looking at something else. It might be time to throw in the towel on this one."*

This is risky (they could walk away, after all) but it does tend to stir people to action.

19.

Handling the Very Needy Customer

Salesperson: *"Hi, LouAnn."*

Prospect: *"Hello, Jeff."*

Salesperson: *"What can I do for you today, LouAnn?"*

Prospect: *"I just wanted to see if they had fixed the broken window in the family room?"*

Salesperson: *"You mean the window you told us about yesterday?"*

Prospect: *"Yes. And I wanted to get a loan update as well."*

Salesperson: *"Well, the superintendent has ordered the new window and will install it as soon as the drywall is hung and the siding is installed; that minimizes the risk of breaking the window all over again. As far as the loan goes, it's <u>still</u> approved and waiting for the home to be finished."*

Prospect: *"Oh. Well, I guess I'll go measure a couple of things in the model."*

Salesperson (Under your breath): *"You mean, you don't have the measurements committed to memory by now?"*

Perhaps you've not had the opportunity to work in an office with cubicles all around you. One of the interesting aspects in such a situation is that you are (whether you like it or not) privy to the trials and ordeals of your co-workers. Now imagine that the person in the cubicle next to yours is, shall we say, of the 'emotional ilk'. And let's say that this person tends to take every event in life as if it is a major trauma. And just to complete the picture, let's assume that this person just bought a brand new home. Guess what – you get to hear her talk about the process for the next *six months!*

Buying a home is a stressful and emotional endeavor, one of the most nerve-racking things we will go through in our entire lifetime. It's like that for anyone, but it is especially trying for those who are detail-oriented and high-strung to start with.

You need to understand how scary this process is to that particular customer. Face it – you see the process of buying a home every day and it might not be that big of a deal to you. The customer goes through this a few times in their entire *life*; it's bound to be a big deal to them. Home-buying is scary, and that's a fact. Don't be surprised when some people react to their fear by inundating themselves with information and hounding you for updates. They want nothing to slip through the cracks.

There is one other consideration here: the customer's expectations. Whether they've purchased a home before or not, many customers have a negative expectation about the purchase process. Perhaps they were forced to endure a horrible transaction on a previous home purchase. Or they are transferring the car buying experience (horrible as it often is) to the homebuying process. Maybe they have a friend or relative who bought a new home and is insisting that the builder be watched like a hawk. In any event, the customer's expectations about the process combined with the degree to which they trust the home-building company will determine how diligent they feel they need to watch over the process. Understand the expectations and you will likely understand how to manage those expectations.

How to handle these sometimes-trying customers?

ASSURE THEM YOU'RE HERE TO HELP

One of the curious things about being a new home sales representative is that you are there to take care of the home*buyer*, but you're getting paid by the home*seller*. Whose side are you on, anyway? Well, both. You need to convince your customer that while you are, in fact, being paid by the seller and you do have a responsibility to look after the seller's interests throughout this transaction, you are nevertheless here to make your customer's homebuying process as smooth and as enjoyable as possible. Let them know – specifically – how you will help.

> *"I will be your eyes and ears on this job. I will walk through your home on a regular basis, I will talk to the on-site superintendent several times a week, and I will track your financing through the approval process. Most importantly, I will call you at least once a week while you're going through this to update you and see if you have any concerns. By the way, I tend to make my update calls on Tuesdays. Does that work for you?"*

STICK TO YOUR PROMISES

Now that you've promised your best service you must deliver on what you've pledged to do. Customers will quickly lose confidence when they find that you (or your co-workers) are not living up to your word. When this happens you can expect that they will take it upon themselves to scrutinize everything that happens in the process.

If you know you cannot come through on a promise by all means let the customer know about it before the promise is broken. If you told the customer that the cabinets are being installed on Friday, but you find out on Friday morning that the cabinets are not going in until Tuesday, don't wait until Monday to let them know. If the customer comes out on Saturday and the cabinets are not installed, your credibility goes out the window. Don't put yourself in this position. Remember, good news never gets better, but bad news always gets worse.

BEAT THEM AT THEIR OWN GAME

Now let's get to the real tough ones, the people who call or come in *almost every day*. While it is possible that some of these buyers are just plain lonely and looking for your companionship, it is more likely that the customer *believes* they need to come in every day in order to ensure that nothing slips through the cracks. The mentality is, "If I want this done right I'm going to have stay on top of these people."

If the real issue is the need to persuade the customer that you are, in fact, on top of things and that you are constantly aware of what's happening with their home and their transaction, you might try beating them at their own game – by calling them incessantly. When someone is calling you literally every day, turn the tables. Make it a point to call them first thing in the morning, *every day for a week*. Start your day by being proactive in calling your customer.

> *"Good morning, it's Jeff. I talked to Steve about the wall in the family room and he says he had already seen the bow, that he has already talked to the framer, and that it should be fixed by the end of the day. I'll check that before I leave today and call you tomorrow morning to let you know that it got taken care of. If you need anything before that, just call."*

The trick is not to do this once, but *every day* for several days. Then notice whether the customer's calls diminish. You are trying to teach your customer that you are already looking at the things they are concerned about, and that it is not necessary to call or come in every day because we are already here and we are looking after the home and the process.

E-MAIL EARLY IN THE DAY

If you have access to e-mail you could consider sending them a brief daily update first thing each morning. Even if you have nothing new to report you are still being proactive, and the 30 seconds it takes to send an e-mail to this person might save you 15 minutes in phone calls or office visits. It doesn't have to be detailed; it only has to be frequent and consistent.

"Walked your home this morning. Looks great – right on schedule. Meeting with mortgage company today. I'll get you an update tomorrow. Jeff"

REMIND THEM THAT YOU HAVE OTHER CUSTOMERS

In the worst-case scenario it might be necessary to politely inform people that you have a great many customers to serve and you need to be able to do that. Be sensitive, apologetic, and contrite.

"I enjoy spending time with you and I really appreciate your diligence in staying on top of the progress. I do need to let you know that we are currently working with twenty different homebuyers and I need to spend time with each one of them. You're welcome to come by every day, but please understand and forgive me when I cannot spend a great deal of time with you on every visit."

One more thing on this subject - a personal lesson that I learned the hard way. I once had a homebuyer (we'll call her Susan) who came into my sales office *every day*. I mean that – every day! It got to the point where I shuddered when she pulled in because I knew she was about to eat up more of my time.

After Susan closed she got a survey from our company. One of the questions on the survey asked, "Did the salesperson keep you informed?" Susan marked "Not at all". I was furious. Sometime later Susan came back into my sales office, looking sheepish.

Susan said, "Jeff, I got this survey and I…"

I interrupted. "And you said I didn't keep you informed. I know – I saw the survey! Susan, how could you say that? I talked to you *every single day!"*

Susan replied, "No, Jeff. I talked to *you* every single day. You never called me one time in the entire six months the home was being built."

Now, you might be thinking to yourself that this was totally unfair and that I got a bum deal (and I'd be thinking that I agree with you). But the lesson was invaluable. The buyer calling us for updates *doesn't count*. The only thing that counts is when we *proactively* call the buyer (and in my opinion each and every week). If you've promised to call the buyer every Tuesday, call them every Tuesday – even if the buyer had been in your office on Monday. The proactivity is what counts.

20.

Demonstrating a Option-Laden Home

Prospect: *"Can you tell me what's upgraded in this model?"*
Salesperson: *"Well, we actually put a lot of upgrades in our models."*
Prospect: *"But surely you can tell me what's extra."*
Salesperson: *"Well, I can…but it might take a while."*
Prospect: *"Would it be quicker for you to tell me what is standard?"*
Salesperson: *"Definitely."*
Prospect: *"Well, go ahead then."*
Salesperson: *"Ummmm…this toilet."*
Prospect: *"You mean that's it? That's the only thing that is standard? The toilet?"*
Salesperson: *"Yes, but not the toilet seat. That's extra."*

Why do homebuilders decorate model homes? Because they watch a lot of HGTV and want to put to use what they've learned? No. Homebuilders spend tens of thousands of dollars to decorate models because they want the customer to be able to see, understand and appreciate what their home *could be.* The model serves to whet the customer's appetite regarding the possibilities.

It is true that this can sometimes serve to confuse matters, but this is why you're there, right? It's up to you to step in and give the customer a clear picture, both of what is and of what could be.

It's a fact that homebuyers are visual people. Visual aids (such as model homes) provide a strong emotional tie for the prospects. When a home is optioned, furnished and decorated in a pleasing manner the customer's imagination becomes involved in the visualization of living in the home.

There is a down side to how visual customers can be. If you have ten floor plans but only two model homes you've probably noticed the trend to sell the modeled homes at a faster pace than the non-modeled homes. Invariably, the two homes that are modeled are the sales leaders in the community. The customer might not be purchasing the home that fits their needs the best (statistically they are probably not), but they are purchasing the home that has the greatest emotional appeal.

Oh, one other minor detail. Options are an outstanding profit opportunity for your company. That's a fact. Savvy homebuilders will always want to sell as many options as possible. When a builder constructs a model home they are not only showing off a model but also showing off the available options.

How do you walk someone through this value discovery process?

DON'T APOLOGIZE

Many sales counselors will begin the model tour with an apology even before they enter the home. It usually sounds something like this:

"Now one of the things we do with our models is load them up with

every available option (and some things that we do not even offer). You need to know that most everything you are going to see does not come in the price of the home."

For those of you who think I'm making that up I assure you I am not. I've heard salespeople use similar introductions during the model demo. In this instance, the sales counselor is not convinced of the value in the home apart from the options, and that message comes across loud and clear to the prospect.

CALL IT THE 'POSSIBILITY HOUSE'

If you do want to offer an introduction to a home that is laden with extras, there is a way to do that in a positive tone. Simply paint the situation in its strongest possible light by letting the customer know that they can, in fact, get this home looking exactly the way they like it. Everyone has an idea of what they are looking for, and we are hoping that our model will match that mental picture. By pointing out that the home is a blank canvas and that the possibilities for creative expression are limitless, you enhance the value of the offering.

"I want to show you what I call the 'Possibility House'. Everyone wants the killer touches, so we've installed them in this home. You can get these things through our design center and have them included in your mortgage. Let's go take a look."

STAY AWAY FROM IRRELEVANT HYPOTHETICALS

One of the more difficult questions we get during the demonstration is this: *"What would this home cost exactly as it is modeled?"* While I understand the reason that a customer would ask the question, you need to seriously consider whether you should provide an answer. Here's why:

The customer simply wants to know what it will cost to 'trick out' the home they are considering purchasing. That makes sense. The problem is that 'trick out' means something totally different to the customer than it did to the decorator. That is, by answering the question you are offering a numeric gauge of the value of the home, even though the customer has no interest in the decorator's version of value.

Let's suppose the model home has granite slab counters, built-in bookcases in the family room, absolutely top-of-the-line carpeting, and a finished bedroom with bath in place of the standard loft. The costs are $8,000, $5,500, $13,800 and $12,700, respectively, for a total of $40,000. But the prospect would be very happy with granite *tiles*, he already has his own bookcases for the family room, he wants a mid-grade Berber carpet, and he has plans to use the loft as a loft. Would it be nice to have some of those things? Sure. Would he want to pay for them? Not a chance. The buyer's question is irrelevant.

It is also dangerous. By answering the question directly you risk planting the seed in the prospect's mind that the home is no longer affordable. As a sales counselor, I specifically asked *not* to be informed of the cost of all the extras in the model. I wanted to plead ignorance.

Try these responses instead of answering the question directly.

"I could look that up for you, but I'm not sure it would answer the real question. You want to know what it takes to make the model look great, correct? The problem is that 'great' is different for every customer. We've had customers that have spent just a few thousand dollars in our design center, and one customer that spent over one hundred thousand between structural changes and upgrades. The average at this community is about 10% of the purchase price, and you can really do a lot with that."

"That is a good question that is tough to answer. This home has everything, even some things we don't offer in the design center. But for perspective sake, the most anyone has spent on options in this community has been X thousand dollars, and their home turned out just like a model."

SELL THE DESIGN BEFORE SELLING THE FEATURES

The greatest fear of the homebuilder is that the customer will become so consumed with what is standard and what is optional that they will miss the design benefits of the home. That's a real problem, because what people should be buying is livability and design ahead of options and upgrades. After all, you could have all the upgrades in the design center thrown in for free, but if the customer hates the floorplan and cannot picture living in the home in comfort you're not going to make that sale.

> *"I'd be happy to answer any questions you might have regarding the options and upgrades, but before we do that let me ask you a question. How does this home feel to you? Do you like the flow and the design of the home?"*

This approach makes sense for two reasons. First, if the customer doesn't really like the layout, what difference does it make how much the options cost? Second, once they are emotionally tied to the floorplan and the livability, the importance of the features lessens, and appropriately so. People should always make the primary decision based on the layout and the design.

21.

Dealing with the Customer's Construction Concerns

Customer: *"The West wall in my dining room is framed crooked."*

Salesperson: *"Actually, the West wall is straight – the East, North and South walls are framed crooked."*

Customer: *"The concrete is cracking."*

Salesperson: *"There are rumors that our gophers are taking steroids."*

Customer: *"There are Domino's Pizza boxes that the construction workers left in my garage."*

Salesperson: *"That's only because McDonald's doesn't deliver."*

Customer: *"I get the sense I would have more luck talking to the superintendent."*

Salesperson: *"Don't do that. He hates it when people wake him up in the middle of the day."*

Ouch! So that example is on the brutal side, but it serves a purpose. In my 20 years in this business I have found a constant and disturbing trend regarding customer satisfaction:

If sales and construction don't get along, the customer suffers.

From time to time I'll get called by a homebuilding company to a training session on customer satisfaction. They want me to get in a room with all the salespeople and all the superintendents and teach them how to be nice to customers. What the company really needs is a class on how to be nice to each other! The level of service that is provided to a customer cannot exceed the quality of the relationship between the sales counselors and the superintendents.

I have preached for years about one single word that can be absolutely devastating when used with a customer. The word is, 'they'. The derivations are 'them', 'those guys in the trailer', and eventually, 'the morons who couldn't schedule a house correctly if their lives depended on it'. You typically hear the terms used in this manner: "They told me the home would be ready on the 15th – I don't know why it got delayed. Talk to them".

As soon as we start talking in 'they' language we are distancing ourselves from 'them'. We are sending the message to the customer that we are not a cohesive team. This is precisely what the customer does *not* want to hear.

My advice to you is to go on a single crusade within your company to get rid of the word 'they' and replace it with 'we'. The best-run companies in the world are 'We' organizations. "When we win, we win together. When we struggle, we struggle together. There is no they only we."

Of course, when you pick up one end of the stick you pick up the other. So being a part of a 'We' organization also means that you are the repository for construction issues and concerns. News flash: that's part of your job! Your customer needs to know that they have an advocate who will listen to their concerns and speak on their behalf. I'm sorry if I sound preachy on this, but I am sick and tired of the 'That's not my job' attitude that I see in so many sales offices. As far as I'm concerned, if it has to do with serving the customer – it's *everyone's job*. Okay, I'll get off the soap box.

Construction concerns are very real and very scary for the customer. An important part of your job is to alleviate their concerns and to assure them that your company takes their concerns seriously. This is not the time to downplay their fears, and it is most certainly not the time to stand behind such underachieving approaches as "industry standards", or worse, "company policy". This is a partnership, the home*buyer* and the home*builder*.

One of the ways that you can demonstrate your concern for the customer is to be thoroughly educated regarding the home they are purchasing. You should be regularly walking the homes that are under construction, and you should not think twice about heading out onsite whenever a specific customer concern arises. If possible, walk the home with your superintendent so that you can have the first-hand explanation at the ready when you call the customer to discuss the concern.

As an added bonus, every construction concern raised by the customer affords you an opportunity to increase your knowledge about the homebuilding process. Take advantage of these times as a way to increase your knowledge and make you more valuable both to your company and to your customers.

Thoughts on handling customer concerns about construction...

LISTEN, LISTEN, LISTEN

A construction concern might be based on an actual construction problem...or it might be based on fear or lack of trust. Homebuyers who don't trust the company or its representatives will feel the need to bring every small item to your attention, for fear that if they do not raise the issue no one else will.

You need to fully understand the issue before you can address it. Ask lots of questions to make sure you are clear on the root causes of the concern. If the customer is 'venting', let them get things off their chest. Listen intently and take lots of notes. This is a scary time. What the customer really needs is a sales counselor who understands what they are going through and will listen to their concerns.

OFFER AN EDUCATION

Sometimes a customer will say something that sounds like a complaint but is really a statement of ignorance. Homebuyers are often unaware of the systems and processes that go into home construction, so the concern might be addressed through a simple explanation. The more the customer understands about the process the more likely it is that they can accept the methods that are being used.

ASK THE CUSTOMER FOR THEIR IDEAL REMEDY

The raising of construction concerns can be seen as a sort of negotiation with the homebuyer. They have an ideal remedy in mind and you need to determine whether that solution is feasible. Don't be afraid to ask.

> *"Thanks for bringing that up. We want to make sure you are comfortable and confident with the construction of your home. Tell me what the ideal remedy would be. How would you like to see this resolved?"*

If the customer comes back with an unrealistic expectation ("tear the house down and start over again") you can counter with the need to find some middle ground.

> *"So what else would be acceptable to you? I want to represent your interests when I meet with the team, so tell me what you are willing to accept as a remedy."*

PROMISE A PROMPT REPLY

When a customer raises a construction concern you must consider it an urgent issue. Even if you know it's trivial in the big picture it is still a major ordeal in the customer's mind. When your customer is going through the process of buying a home – especially a newly built home – they are consumed with the details. These details keep people up at night. Remember that customers are not concerned because they don't have all the answers; they are anxious because they don't even know the right questions.

Alleviate their concerns by giving them a specific target date for resolution – then get back to them well before the deadline. If you think you can get the situation resolved by noon tomorrow, say:

"I understand your concern and we're going to get right on it. Give me a chance to talk to the right people. I'll have an answer for you by the end of the day tomorrow. Fair enough?"

RETURN THE CALL WITH THE SUPERINTENDENT ON THE PHONE

Familiarity breeds...comfort, especially in dealings between a homebuyer and a superintendent. Getting your customer to trust the builder is a huge step in helping them to alleviate their fears. When a customer connects directly with the superintendent a greater sense of trust ensues. No longer is the superintendent some guy with an attitude who is only concerned about passing inspections. The customers can hear first hand that the superintendent is a real person with real standards, someone who cares about the quality of the home.

Remember that this is a very scary process for the homebuyer. What they need more than anything else is an advocate.

About the Author

Jeff Shore is a contemporary expert in the area of new home sales and sales management. He proudly admits to being a "sales junkie" and his passion is in bringing out the best in homebuilding professionals. His philosophy: Great Results Come from Great People!

The former National Sales Director for KBHome, Jeff is a student of sales first and a teacher second. His leadership is far from theoretical – Jeff started his new home career as a sales representative in Northern California where he sold in excess of 500 homes. He moved up to Vice President of Sales and Marketing for a 1,000+ unit homebuilding division, overseeing a sales staff of 35. He went on to a corporate position where he wrote and delivered training programs, coached managers and directed sales strategy.

Today, the Shore Company provides strategy and training services to homebuilding companies large and small across the country. With solid experience combined with a theatre arts background, Jeff delivers training programs that have been described as "extremely powerful", "a lot of fun" and "very, very practical."

Jeff Shore resides in Auburn, California with his wife, Karen, their three children, and two neurotic Jack Russell Terrorists.

Visit www.jeffshore.com, or send an e-mail to jeff@jeffshore.com.